Divisiveness and Social Conflict

Divisiveness and Social Conflict

AN ANTHROPOLOGICAL APPROACH

Alan R. Beals and Bernard J. Siegel

1966
STANFORD UNIVERSITY PRESS
Stanford, California

Stanford University Press
Stanford, California
© *1966 by the Board of Trustees of the*
Leland Stanford Junior University
Printed in the United States of America
L.C. 66-17560

To Constance and Charlotte

Preface

This book is the outcome of a dialogue, carried on between the authors for several years, on the nature of factional dispute and its relation to other forms of conflict. Our dialogue began informally, as dialogues do, and at first focused on descriptions of factionalist episodes—their onset, the parties to the dispute, their escalation, and so forth—in the two communities, widely separated in space and history, we had between us studied. In the course of exploring the problem, we discovered a mutual concern with the nature of process in social behavior and with certain insights into society and culture that may be gained by attending to process phenomena.

We do not pretend to offer a systematic theory of conflict or even of divisiveness, nor do we suggest a novel concept of culture that will serve directly to construct a more adequate theory of culture than now exists. However, we hope that as our argument develops, it will provide some new insights relevant to these tasks, or at least will reinforce certain concepts over others in the literature. We view conflict not simply as a domain in itself, but also as a manifestation of the inherent properties of culturally based behavior in its continuing interaction with the environment. In this sense our approach is ecological. It explicitly relates the dynamics of external conditions—the multifold operations of the environment—to customary adaptations of belief systems and social structure.

It is perhaps surprising that until recently there were few anthropological contributions to the substantial body of literature on conflict processes. One of the most important sources of conflict situations lies in the domain of law; anthropological studies are beginning to clarify certain major attributes of this domain, thereby making legal phenomena more amenable to comparative analysis. We also encounter in the literature functional interpretations of customs that are thought to control the social tensions generated by certain institutions, such as segmentary lineage systems, hereditary claims to privileges (in certain chiefdoms), and oppositions among moieties or castes. "Rituals of rebellion," Gluckman suggests (1963, chap. 3), constitute one class of tension-reducing customs. As yet anthropologists have not dealt much with the question of incomplete problem-solving in cultural adaptation, or with the sources of conflict that, theoretically, are intrinsic to the role of culture in human behavior.

Several facts about the development of anthropological investigations help account for this relative lack of emphasis on social and cultural processes. First, anthropological inquiry has typically preferred the more stable groups and situations to the less stable. In recently colonial areas—in Africa, for example—the politically dominant Europeans had established situations stable enough that anthropologists could profitably deal with the surviving "tribal" societies as if they were autonomous. With a few exceptions, the public reports of such research contained chapters giving a historical overview of the region and observations about certain changes caused by culture-contact. Many fewer reports were specifically concerned with describing the phenomena of change. Even studies of remnant societies, like the ethnographies of certain American Indian tribes, attempted to reconstruct an earlier and more stable era from the memories of the oldest informants.

Second, a substantial part of this enterprise, especially in England, derived theoretically, by way of Radcliffe-Brown, from Emile Durkheim and French sociology. The aim of this school was to analyze enough societies, structurally and functionally, in sufficient depth to make valid comparison and generalization possible. It conceived culture as consisting of those customary rules, abstracted from behavior (including verbal behavior) by the observer, that, when expressed in beliefs, define the relationship system. This is, in other words, a normative system which views society as approximating a state of equilibrium, that is, as exhibiting a considerable degree of harmony or internal consistency. Cleavage in one situation will be matched by alliance in another. One class of relationships will imply others; over time one set of forces will equal and offset other, conflicting forces. This concept of culture makes some place, but in very special terms, for the fact that rules cannot always apply as they should and that people will not always behave as they ought. In a lineage-based society, demographic processes can extinguish any given segment in a generation. Certain kinsmen may, or may be thought to, behave inappropriately toward other classes of kinsmen. Nevertheless, whenever the functioning of the system is disturbed, a society will have the means to redress the situation, to return it to a "steady state," to relieve tensions in ways that enable the relationship system to operate in its normal mode. Besides Gluckman's views on the functions of certain classes of rituals, various interpretations of witchcraft customs have been expressed in these terms. All of these analyses operate on the premise that societies must be in a stable condition, or trying to return to such a state, in order to survive. Our observations lead us to assert that, despite necessary regularities, cultural adaptation at all times contains the seeds of disruption. Opposing forces are not always equal or complementary, nor are they inexorably moving in that direction.

Finally, anthropologists have most often had to work among groups whose history is relatively sketchy about the pertinent social facts they wish to study. It has thus seldom been possible to judge the extent to which an observed or abstracted structure represents a stable system or how long it has maintained essentially its present form. Under these circumstances it is difficult to determine, given a conflict that may be deeply rooted in past experience, whether the method by which it is handled represents an established pattern for coping with consciously recognized implications of certain roles, or whether this method represents ineffective coping with insufficiently articulated ambiguities in the role system.

We believe that if anthropologists and their colleagues in other behavioral sciences will turn their attention away from functionalist assumptions to a less biased analysis of events and their onset, progression, and outcome, we shall in time resolve these problems of stability and adaptability, and, incidentally, develop a more appropriate view of order in society and culture. We concur with Fallers (1956) and Turner (1957), who have expressed themselves most explicitly along these lines.

We are indebted to the Wenner-Gren Foundation and to the National Science Foundation for grants-in-aid that supported field work at Taos and Picuris pueblos, and to the Social Science Research Council for a fellowship that made possible the field work in the Indian village we have called "Namhalli." We also wish to express our gratitude to Robert C. North, Director of Studies in International Conflict and Integration at Stanford, who offered much good advice in the initial stages of this project and who made available a grant-in-aid to help us finish the manuscript. Of the many anthropological colleagues whose work has influenced our thinking, we wish especially to mention Victor W. Turner. We have benefited both from considered examination of his published work and from extended personal discussion. We are also grateful to the many scholars who have been kind enough to respond to our earlier publications. Their comments on their own investigations and analyses of factionalist dispute among a variety of groups helped us to sort out what is conceptually and empirically comparable from the increasing body of case studies, and encouraged us to bring our analysis to its present state. Of course, the responsibility for any errors in interpretation, or for lack of enough good sense to modify certain of our judgments in the light of well-considered criticism, must rest entirely with ourselves.

Finally, we owe more than we can say to the efficient managers of conflict in that most important of political units, the matripotestal family. To them, who have helped so much to make our work a pleasure, we dedicate this book.

A. R. B.

B. J. S.

Contents

Divisiveness and Social Conflict

1. *Organizations and Conflict*

Human organizations have many purposes and perform many tasks. In the family, the factory, or the kingdom, there are times when purposes seem forgotten and tasks are not performed. People quarrel, question each other's motives, disagree concerning the discharge of obligations, indicate lack of interest, or quit the organization. In the hospital patients are not tended as carefully as they once were; in the village crops are not harvested properly; in the factory machines stand idle; in the university classrooms stand empty; and in the kingdom there is disorder and dismay. "Divisiveness" or "divisive conflict" are the terms used here to describe those varieties of conflict that the membership of an organization regards as detrimental and as requiring remedial action.

The following discussion has been guided and directed by research experience in two widely separated communities: Taos Pueblo in New Mexico and Namhalli in South India. Both these settlements have had a history of approaching various major problems through internecine conflict rather than cooperation. The discovery of similarities between these two communities and, later, of the similarity of the patterns of divisive conflict observed there to patterns reported elsewhere led us to the formulation of a preliminary theory concerning the origin and nature of divisive conflict. In attempting to develop such a theory, we have derived abundant assistance from the works of Simmel (1955), Bateson (1935, 1958), Coser (1956, 1957), Gluckman (1939), Sorokin (1937), and Turner (1957). Many of the approaches outlined here have parallels in the literature of political science, sociology, business administration, and social psychology. We have attempted to reconcile divergent views, to toss out such false issues as the functional significance of conflict, and to introduce an element of order into the problem of defining terms and stating propositions.

ORGANIZATIONS

An organization or cultural system consists of a succession of sets of human beings who interact within and between sets with sufficient frequency to establish an identifiable boundary. When such interaction takes place, problems are identified and solved, boundaries are maintained, and traditional ways of doing things are established and modified. From an evolutionary or developmental standpoint, the formation of an organization commences as soon as two or more people recognize each other's existence and begin to interact. How the duration and intensity of such interaction affects the character of organizations has yet to be clearly described, but it is possible to recognize important differences between such things as a hospital in which the staff is nonresident and the patients transient, and a mental or chronic-disease hospital in which patients live for long periods in association with a resident staff. That laboratory groups, societies, factories, schools, tribes, nations, villages, and families are different is undeniable. At the same time, there is no evidence that they differ so radically as to require a different body of theory for each. We prefer to assume that theories of divisive conflict can be applied to all such groups with only a few systematic variations. All are equally human organizations; all involve the same processes of decision making, problem finding, communicating, cooperating, and disputing.

Probably the most effective way to establish a typology of organizations will involve consideration of the kinds of boundaries actually established and considered by investigators to be relevant to particular research problems. Organizations are natural units, but things in nature do not come packed in neat little boxes. It is up to the student to define the organization he is studying, preferably according to rigorously specified criteria. Residential communities such as Taos and Namhalli have a great many distinct boundaries of various kinds, and therefore may usefully illustrate the problems involved in defining and describing organizational boundaries.

Namhalli is located on a rolling plain near the city of Bangalore in Mysore State. The village consists of a group of houses situated on a rectangle of land. There has been a village named Namhalli on roughly this same patch of land for at least 160 years, and the ruins of an earlier village testify to an even longer occupation. To accomplish this perpetuation, the villagers have fought off bandits, rapacious government officials, famines, and epidemics without at any one time greatly altering the normal and characteristic patterns that make Namhalli completely and uniquely Namhalli. There was a time when Namhalli did not exist, and, in a few decades, when Namhalli is absorbed by the growing city of Bangalore, it may possibly cease to exist. Namhalli represents a bounded patch of territory and a bounded patch of time.

Taos has been in existence for many hundreds of years, although it once occupied a site several miles away from its present location. During the years that the Taoseños have dwelt on the valley floor near the Sangre de Cristo mountains of New Mexico, they have had to cope with the incursions of various groups, the most recent of whom have been Spanish-speaking and then English-speaking immigrants, including writers and artists who have settled permanently within what had been regarded as community territory. As a place, Taos is now different from what it once was. In time, it has altered the character of its productive activities, value emphases have changed, and parts of its cultural inventory have been added or subtracted. Nonetheless, despite a long period of interaction with others and many vicissitudes, Taos remains a distinctive entity geographically and temporally defined. By virtue of a common language, common experience, continual resolution of social problems unique to the pueblo, and commitment to aspects of belief and behavior that make permanent residence in other communities difficult or impossible for most of its members, Taos, too, represents a bounded patch of both territory and time.

Not all organizations possess such strongly defined temporal and spatial boundaries as Namhalli and Taos. Infantry companies and harvesting crews, for example, have much less easily defined times and places of interaction. If interaction is to define an organization, there must be definable times and places when such interaction takes place. Equally there must be specific persons who interact at such organizationally significant times and places. As people enter and leave Namhalli by birth and death, by immigration and emigration, their behavior changes sufficiently to permit them to become members of the community. The child is trained to identify and to address other members of the village properly. The young bride is punished when she fails to make the identifications and conform to the behaviors appropriate to a young bride entering into community membership. Persons who repeatedly engage in behavior that is contrary to the Namhalli standard may be escorted to the geographical boundary and told never to return. Historically, when the community failed to reproduce its population biologically, steps were taken to increase the membership through recruiting. And when the population of the community became too large, steps were taken to transfer the excess population elsewhere or to expand community resources. The range of behavior that is identified as organizationally significant is very wide, but there are occasions upon which the individual member may behave in a manner that one may call irrelevant to the organization. In Namhalli, the parents of a young man may choose for him a bride who is hard-working and homely rather than one who is less hard-working but attractive, or they may choose a bride who speaks either the Kannada or Telegu languages. The organization does possess detailed customs concerning exogamy, endogamy, and a host of other features that regulate the prospective bride's behavior, but within defined limits variations in individual behavior are organizationally irrelevant.[1] The situation at Taos is similar except that there has been very little immigration, the membership being acquired almost entirely by birth.

In an organization such as the local chapter of the Rotary Club,

[1] From a psychological viewpoint, the concept of "indifference" formulated by Simmel (1955, p. 14) appears to parallel the more sociological concept of irrelevance. Presumably indifference is the individual's response to irrelevance.

the range of behavior regarded as irrelevant is much greater than in small residential communities, yet even here the impact of organizational participation upon individual behavior is marked, as is the perpetuation of the behavior regardless of changes in membership. Human beings create organizations and, far more than is sometimes suspected, engage in deliberate planning and discussion concerning the kinds of traditions and rituals they wish to have and the kinds of changes they wish to make. But not just any person does these things. They are done by the membership, by those people who have already indicated general agreement with organizational goals and activities by engaging in appropriate behavior. Organizations influence people, and people create fresh organizational materials, in a never-ending cycle. Personality reigns supreme only in an evolutionary and historical context where we may speak (possibly without too much justification) of uncultured primates coming together to create human organizations.

The ancient conflicts between free will and predestination, between the great man theory and the superorganic, that is, between the cults of personality and culturology, are irresolvable. Human beings are neither slaves of culture nor free agents; they are somewhere in between. It is a fallacy to argue that human beings must be either slave or free. We must speak of a constant tension between conformity to organizationally approved behavior, performance of irrelevant behavior, and nonconformity. The individual who fails to perform relevant behaviors or who overindulges in nonconformity will cease to be included within organizational boundaries. Although in a sense an organization *is* its membership, there is also a sense in which the collective membership operates upon individuals to transform them into members or nonmembers. The term "society" can be used in its restricted sense to refer to the membership of an organization, to those behaviors that are characteristic of the membership, or to relationships among members. When used in such a manner, "society" does not include boundary relationships that organizations maintain between themselves and those aspects of their environment that are not human or that are not included in membership categories. Such relationships are perhaps best included under the term "ecology."

Virtually everything that may in some sense be considered part of the surroundings of Namhalli reflects the influence of its presence, the establishment of an ecology. The soil of the village fields is a product of years of plowing, harvesting, manuring, and planting. The crops grown in the fields are a product of years of selection; the animals in the village streets have been bred, fed, and trained in such a way as to reflect in some degree the community of Namhalli. Thousands of years into the future, the special qualities that are Namhalli will persist, although in ever-lessening degree, in the soil, the vegetation, and all other immediate surroundings. The buildings, equipment, and artifactual materials owned and used by the members of Namhalli reflect even more the characteristics of the village, and by their nature exert a continuing influence on the behavior of successive members.

Taos, in traditional times, could almost be said to have constructed its own environment. The vegetation and wildlife surrounding Taos must have been very different before the pueblo was established, and archeologists have affirmed the persistence of Taos's impact upon its environment. Although some organizations, such as a bomber crew or a bridge club, affect their environment in ways that are difficult to define, we would argue that organizations have a definite impact upon the persons and things that surround them, to a degree varying from the trivial to the irreversible. When organizational behavior is directed toward the solution or handling of particular problems, it tends to develop a characteristic pattern, and so forms a boundary between the organization and the environment.

THE NATURE OF ORGANIZATIONS

The boundary of an organization is not a line on a map; it is not a negative incline on an interaction diagram; it is not a recognition of the fact that the organization exists. A boundary includes these things, but it is also the total product of the influence of successive sets of members upon one another and upon everything with which they have come in contact. Theories that make distinctions among fancied physical, biological, and social environments are more concerned with history than with organizational behavior. If we are concerned with organizations, the important characteristic of an outside influence is its effect on the organization. Stating that such and such an influence is physical, biological, or social says nothing about its impact. The influence of the external worlds of Namhalli, Taos, or any other organization is best described in terms of those characteristic behaviors that establish an identifiable boundary between the organization and the outside world. The consistency of such boundary relationships is a result of the establishment of a cultural tradition.

The cultural tradition

The members of Namhalli and Taos are continually influencing the thought and behavior of their fellow members. Most of this influence takes place directly: members observe the activity of other members; members tell other members what to do; members indicate disapproval when rules are broken. Some influence takes place indirectly. In Namhalli, the child's hands curve to fit the plow handle, not because he was told or taught to curve his hands, but because the plow handle has had the same characteristic shape for generations. Long-dead ancestors chose the site of Namhalli (high enough to escape the mosquitoes, low enough to be near water), determined which men might live there ("We study each man's character; if he is a good man we offer him land, if he is a bad man we ask him to leave the village"), and throughout many generations made progressive alterations of the environment that influence the behavior of Namhalli's membership. In Taos, where citizenship is determined largely by birth and only to a small extent by marriage, the influence of ancestors and neighbors, and of intensive communication within a small, clearly defined group, is even more marked. The continuity of life and the orderliness of daily activity in Namhalli and Taos, as in other organizations, stems from the fact that all members are recipients in whole or in part of a complex set of messages passed down from previous members and exchanged among present members. It is these messages transmitted through persons and through the environment that constitute the cultural tradition of an organization.

A cultural tradition may be identified in terms of certain characteristic behavior that the membership exhibits in maintaining organizational boundaries and in terms of the influences that pass from one member of the organization to another. When the child in Namhalli runs into his house and demands rice, his mother tells him that rice is not suitable food for active people. Strong and healthy people eat millet. In time, the child becomes a lean, well-muscled eater of millet rather than a plump rice eater. When a child in Taos enters the house to partake of a festival meal, either parent will kindly but firmly put him aside to wait until all adults and guests are served. It is shameful and disrespectful to insist upon eating first, and the habit of patient waiting soon becomes routine. Although the children's behavior in these two cases may be said to be directed by the behavior of their parents, the parental behavior is not unique, but stereotyped. In a sense it was not the parent as a person who caused the child to receive the relevant cultural message, just as it was not in the power of the child as a person to refuse to receive the message. The parents did what any parents in Namhalli, or in Taos, would do. The messages to the children were not the result of any particular decision; the response was automatic: "Our people do not eat rice except on special occasions," or "We wait until adults and guests are served."

Even if parents were determined to swim against the stream and, in Namhalli, feed the child rice or, in Taos, set a special table so that children could eat before guests, they would stand little chance against the combined pressures of mothers-in-law, neighbors, and so on. In Namhalli, other members of the household would have refused to let the mother have rice for her spoiled child; in Taos, the impatient child would not have been allowed inside a neighbor's home to visit. All this is part of the cultural tradition, which itself determines that there shall be mothers-in-law, husbands, neighbors, and mothers, to say nothing of village headmen and priests. It defines the manner in which persons playing these roles shall influence persons playing other roles.

Were cultural traditions the sole determinants of human behavior, human beings could be regarded as mere automata responding without will to the cultural messages transmitted to them through other human beings and the environment. But this could be true only if the information or stimulation affecting the human individual were limited entirely to cultural materials and if cultural materials were unaffected by entropy. This condition could be achieved only by a cultural tradition that successfully rendered predictable everything that happened within its environment, and included an appropriate response for every conceivable variation of human genetic materials, for the manifold problems of birth and death, growth and decay, and for the changing configurations of the physical, biological, and social characteristics of the external world.

The unexpected

In Namhalli and in Taos, messages and influences received by the ordinary person do not inevitably fall within the limits of tradition. Cultural messages from other villages and societies daily cross community boundaries. Genetic messages pass from parents to children in the lottery of birth. Cumulus clouds move across the sky, and rain sometimes falls where and when it is expected to fall, and sometimes does not. In time, attempts to explain these conflicting messages become woven into the cultural traditions, and thus the people come to believe that the cultural message contains explanations for all of the significant things that unpredictably happen across the community boundary to produce rice eaters in a village that should consist of millet eaters or to produce conflict where there should be only peaceful and well-intentioned people. Obviously, the cultural tradition is never transmitted perfectly from one person to another, and even if it were, the many other influences would prevent absolute conformity to the teachings and doings of the forefathers.[2]

But since the unexpected is always with us, cultural traditions are continually being modified. The boundary of Namhalli has

---

[2] The following comment upon predictability is interesting in this connection: " 'Do you realize,' he asked, 'that the whole purpose of civilization is to take the surprises out of life, so one can be bored to death? That a culture in which nothing unexpected ever happens is in what is called its "golden age"?' " (Leinster, 1957, p. 21.)

changed many times, but it never breaks or disappears.[3] In one
sense the Namhalli of 1850 was completely different from the Namhalli of 1960, but in another sense the two Namhallis are the same
village, for as one traces the history of Namhalli, it is impossible to
say when the Namhalli of 1850 ceased to exist or when the Namhalli of 1960 came into being. The tradition of Namhalli has
changed to include portions of other traditions and to accommo-
date new outside forces and influences that were not present in
1850. From one point of view, it can be said that the people of
Namhalli have brought about these changes in the tradition, but
it is also true that they merely transmitted external pressures that
modified the tradition.

In Taos, the physical boundaries, according to the archeological
evidence, definitely changed several hundred years ago, when
Coronado and the Spanish entered the village in 1540. The boundary was then much as it is today, although it has shrunk somewhat
in recent times as land has been lost to the Spanish and Anglos. The
less tangible boundaries of Taos have also altered with the introduction of new crops, occupations, and skills, and with the teaching of English and Spanish as secondary languages. Subtle changes
can thus be identified in almost every aspect of the cultural tradition, but in fundamental ways Taoseños remain the same as their
forebears, and it remains possible to identify a unique and characteristic cultural tradition.

Beliefs

In Namhalli and Taos, a system of beliefs defines the character
of the organizational boundary, and describes the various circumstances and objects that exist and are relevant to it, including the
manner of their existence and their special qualities. Inextricably
linked to the belief system is a set of values, policy conditions,[4] or
goals that specify the desirability or undesirability of the circumstances and objects defined by the belief system. Within the frame-

[3] The problem of boundary definition appears to have received little attention,
but see Mills (1964, pp. 70, 111).
[4] See North, Koch, and Zinnes (1960, p. 356) for a discussion of "policy conditions" and also for an interesting method of analyzing communications between opposed groups.

work of perceptions and motives provided by the belief and value systems is a behavioral system that specifies appropriate behaviors under the various circumstances that are recognized.[5] In Taos, where the boundary between the organization and the external world is strongly and consciously defined, it is felt that all citizens should strive for perfect agreement on all public issues, and that traditionally qualified individuals should have the power to enforce consensus and to terminate conflict with a heavy hand. It is felt that all noncitizens should be treated with suspicion and restraint, that relationships between citizens and noncitizens should be limited to specific activities, and that conversation with outsiders should be restricted to topics considered harmless by Taoseños.

Because the belief system contained within a particular cultural tradition is not reality, but merely a set of attempts to describe reality, the meaning of events does not necessarily derive directly from their nature. When a citizen of Namhalli looks across the fields on a hot day and sees light reflections caused by air turbulence, he invariably describes them with a term translatable as "heat horses." The citizen of Taos does not look across fields but rather across a series of patches of land that he distinguishes in terms of the rights that various people exercise over them. In both cases, behavior is based, in varying degrees, upon what the citizen has been taught to perceive when exposed to a particular situation. All human behavior is to some extent conditioned by cultural traditions, and when a person acts as a member of an organization, he acts within a reality defined by the cultural tradition of the organization.

The people of Namhalli and Taos possess hereditary predispositions that affect their perception and their behavior. Such things as birth order, position in social hierarchies, travel, and migration

---

[5] The term "system" is used with two different meanings. In the sense of cultural or social system, it refers to a dynamic entity that has a finite impact upon the persons and things affected by it. In the sense of belief system or value system it refers to an analytic construct that exists only as an aspect of a cultural system. It might be more sensible to divide the functioning of a cultural system into its belief aspect, value aspect, and behavior aspect, but we yield to common usage.

also have an effect that may be considered independent of the effect of a cultural tradition. If separate factors are listed, and the contribution of each to the behavior of persons in the two communities is considered, the obvious patterning of events soon vanishes in a welter of individual causes, some historical, some biological, some social, and some environmental. Although consideration of the effect of some particular factor may, in certain contexts, be of great theoretical value, it is of little or no value if the theoretical goal is the prediction of behavior within a particular community. The impact of the total environment upon the community is mediated by the cultural tradition. The function of the cultural traditions of Namhalli and Taos can thus, in a way, be said to be that of reconciling divergent external influences and rendering them predictable.

Any approach that considers only the influence of external factors upon an organization, but not the nature of the perceptions and solutions that are offered by the cultural tradition, will have limited predictive value. If, for example, it is argued that from time to time biological inheritance will produce a mute, inglorious Milton, a Savonarola, or a potential atomic physicist in the streets of Namhalli or the corridors of Taos, it must be recognized that the chiefs and leaders of these communities are enabled by their cultural tradition to send such deviants packing. The cultural tradition is not just another factor influencing human behavior, for it weaves all such factors into a largely coherent system. Unexpected things happen, and they produce changes. The interpretation of the unexpected, and consequently the kinds of changes that take place, are conditioned by the set of beliefs included within the cultural tradition. The screening of outside happenings through the perceptual net of the belief system ensures continuity of the cultural tradition and of the organization as a whole.

Goals and solutions

Unexpected happenings very often constitute problems that must be solved if the organization is to survive, and the cultural tradition must provide the means of guarding against unpredicted behavior stimulated by unexpected happenings. To the individual, the predictability of fellow members of the organization is just as important as the predictability of other aspects of his surroundings. The cultural tradition can guard against unpredicted behavior and events by providing, among other things, the cognitive materials necessary to reinterpret apparently unpredicted behavior and to explain unexpected happenings. The system of beliefs and rules also accomplishes this, as noted previously, by defining large classes of behavior as irrelevant.

In Namhalli, no one particularly cares whether or not a vegetarian goes to the city and eats meat, or whether a person of low status patronizes a high-status hotel or temple in the city; but if such a person boasted publicly of his exploits or attempted to do the same thing in Namhalli, he would be beaten, for such overt actions *are* of organizational significance. In the same way, the behavior of a man working as a carpenter outside Taos does not matter unless it in some way affects his performance of religious or mutual-aid duties at home. Not all organizations include so wide a range of behaviors within their sphere of traditional concern as a community. A bomber crew, to use an earlier example, is concerned with the behavior of its members only on certain limited and specific occasions. When a crew is in flight, the behavior of the members is organizationally meaningful and almost entirely controlled by the tradition of the crew and of the Air Force. At other times crew members participate in other organizations and follow behaviors appropriate to those organizations.

An organization is perpetuated because its members achieve, or believe they achieve, certain goals or values that could not be achieved as well if they ceased to be members. Even those who become members of an organization involuntarily and at great cost are, by participating in the affairs of the organization, tacitly admitting that continued participation is the most practical alternative open to them at the moment. In old Namhalli, servants who ran away were brought back to the village and severely punished. As individuals, such servants evidently did not agree, either consciously, or unconsciously, with the majority of the population, but since few were able to make good their escape, they came to accept organizational participation as an optimal strategy.

Clearly, the public and formal goals of an organization cannot be achieved by all members. In Namhalli, members of the lowest caste eat beef in violation of one of the principal rules of the community. In many ways, the role of the lowest caste is that of the witch or subversive, who consciously or unconsciously opposes formal organizational goals. Nevertheless, members of the lowest caste tend to believe that ordinary members of the community should *not* eat beef or indulge in similar rule-breaking activities, and they are quick to spread derogatory rumors about those who adopt their own anti-organizational behaviors. Thus, although the lowest caste is formally excluded from many of the rewards of organizational membership and fails to share all of the goals of the membership at large, they continue to support the community. In Taos, those who have had insufficient kiva training are excluded from the tribal council. Although many of these men complain about what they consider to be an arbitrary restriction, thus showing a certain rejection of organizational goals, they continue to participate in group affairs and to abide by council decisions.

In the Mayan village of Chan Kom (Redfield, 1962), the community publicly decided to "choose progress." Such an explicit statement of goals is common, but it may or may not have much to do with actual goals. It may, for example, be an intellectual counterweight within a complicated and contradictory system of beliefs and values. People in Namhalli express a strong consensus that concern with day-to-day problems of survival is spiritually undesirable, but since they also believe that this state of unconcern is attainable only after many rebirths, they continue to busy themselves mainly with these mundane problems.

All this should indicate very clearly that there are grave problems involved in the definition of community goals. Often, goals center about the continuation of certain standard activities that are characteristic of the organization. Where the goals that people *say* they have differ sharply from what they actually seem to seek or to achieve, a question arises whether the actual behavior represents a real goal or simply a failure to achieve the stated goal. We think that most of the things done by members within an organizational context will be fairly easily identifiable in terms of the achievement of both stated goals and "actual" goals. For the most part, then, divisiveness can be described either in terms of the fact that members regard conflict as detrimental to the achievement of organizational goals or in terms of the fact that it constitutes an interruption of the ongoing task and requires third-party intervention. Where there exists an element of "muddle," so that it becomes difficult to distinguish between competition and divisiveness, it can be argued that this lack of clarity is itself an indication that divisiveness rather than competition or favorably regarded conflict is involved.

SYMBOLS AND OPPOSITIONS

Ideally, the functioning of an organization consists of the interaction of its membership with one another and with an environment in order to achieve organizational goals. Because people do not always know what organizational goals are, or disagree over the part they are to play in achieving them, the functioning of an organization always implies failures of cooperation and mechanisms for dealing with the problems created by such failures. The failure of things to work out properly may lead to recriminations, but this does not necessarily mean that failures of cooperation are conflict. The members of an organization are concerned not so much with the success of every cooperative venture as with doing things in the proper way and in the right spirit. In other words, the consequences of a fellow member's action are less important than its meaning.

When the housewife in Namhalli emerges from her house at sunup, she is likely to see the housewife next door sweeping the street in front of her house. This activity symbolizes a concern with such organizational goals as getting up early, being industrious, and being a good housekeeper. Had the neighbor been sweeping

the street in front of the first housewife's door, the latter would
have thought her neighbor was stealing cow dung—and thus expressing her opposition toward her neighbor and her rejection of
such community goals as harmony and honesty. Had the neighbor
merely been standing in front of her house admiring the sunrise,
it would have meant relatively little and would very likely have
been dismissed as organizationally irrelevant behavior.

We argue, then, that every action by a member of an organization conveys a definite meaning to other members—reflecting irrelevance, assistance, or opposition.[6] In the case above, where the
housewife shows her opposition by stealing cow dung, the first
housewife has a choice of responses. If the neighbor is wealthy and
powerful, she may reply to the expression of opposition with an
expression of assistance, or she may simply ignore it. But if the two
housewives are of approximately equal status, the woman whose
cow dung is being stolen may best conform to organizational goals
by showing opposition to her nieghbor. She may do this by a verbal
harangue calculated to draw an audience, or she may seize her
broom and give her opponent a sound drubbing. If the victimized
housewife herself has a reputation for stealing cow dung, her best
strategy for showing conformity to organizational goals might be
to ignore the intruder and the signaled opposition.

In Taos it once came to the attention of the membership that
two persons from the same family had talked freely to a stranger
about certain customs of the pueblo that were considered secret,
and that these secrets had subsequently been made public outside
the pueblo. Because the two persons who thus showed opposition
to pueblo goals were members of a high-ranking family, individual
Taoseños were faced with the problem of how to respond to the

[6] G. H. Mead considers the fundamental motives to be those leading to "social
cooperation" and those leading to "social antagonism" (1959, pp. 303–4).
Gluckman considers all social relationships to have two aspects, which he
defines as fission and fusion (1939, p. 168). Simmel's discussion (1955, p. 17),
as usual, is the most inspired: "We designate as 'unity' the consensus and concord of interacting individuals as against their discords, separations, and dis-
harmonies. But we also call 'unit' the total group-synthesis of persons, energies, and forms, that is, the ultimate wholeness of that group, a wholeness
which covers both strictly-speaking unitary relations and dualistic relations."

transgression. A few were openly critical of the offenders, but community officials, afraid of rocking the Establishment, ignored the affair completely. Had those who first expressed opposition by revealing secret information been persons of lower rank, the officials would have shown strong counteropposition in the form of severe punishment or even expulsion.

A more common case at Taos takes place when two persons come at the same time to turn water into their irrigation channels. One of the two is clearly signalling opposition, since family and individual rights to water are carefully scheduled, but regardless of who was at fault, a young man would be expected to defer without protest to an older man. Men of similar status might argue at length and come close to blows. The decision to respond to behavior symbolizing opposition by signalling counteropposition, by signalling assistance, or by ignoring the behavior may be supposed to rest largely upon the second person's over-all assessment of the situation. In this connection, Simmel (1955, p. 19) remarks:

For instance, the opposition of a member to an associate is no purely negative social factor, if only because such opposition is often the only means for making life with actually unbearable people at least possible. If we did not even have the power and the right to rebel against tyranny, arbitrariness, moodiness, tactlessness, we could not bear to have any relation to people from whose characteristics we thus suffer. We would feel pushed to take desperate steps—and these, indeed, would end the relation but do *not*, perhaps, constitute "conflict." Not only because of the fact (though it is not essential here) that oppression usually increases if it is suffered calmly and without protest, but also because opposition gives us inner satisfaction, distraction, relief, just as do humility and patience under different psychological conditions.

In the case of the cow dung thief of high status, or in the two cases at Taos where the person expressing opposition was of high status, it is evident that the fun of responding to an opposition with an opposition had to be weighed against the rather serious consequences if conflict developed. Perhaps the willingness of people in Namhalli and Taos to suffer tyranny gladly derives, in part, from the existence of more or less clearly defined rights and obligations that tend to militate against the increase of oppression.

CONFLICT

Conflict exists when two parties belonging to the same organization exchange behaviors that symbolize opposition. As defined here, "conflict" must always involve organizationally significant behavior. The terms "fighting" and "warfare" might well be reserved for those cases, if any, where opponents do each other physical injury outside of any system of rules and meanings. In the case of the cow dung theft in Namhalli, the presence of conflict is symbolized when the two women begin beating each other with brooms or when they begin exchanging particular epithets. A stranger, unfamiliar with the rules, might suppose that the two women were playing a game, for there are many cultures in which the act of beating with a broom would have little significance. In Namhalli, where a broom symbolizes pollution and filth, broom-beating calls for immediate third-party intervention. Were the two women merely competing to see which could sweep the largest portion of the street fastest, the exchange of oppositions between the two women would not signify opposition to organizational goals. As Simmel (1955, p. 61) says, competition is the case where "a man fights another man, but *for* a third one."

Some writers tend to define conflict in terms of the existence of scarce goods. Coser (1956, p. 201), for example, says, "if within any social structure, there exists an excess of claimants over opportunities for adequate reward, there arises strain and conflict." Such a definition of conflict seems to us to involve needless complexities. Before we can offer our own definition of conflict, however, we must determine what is meant by scarce goods in each society, and we must somehow explain how scarce goods can be responsible on one occasion for the development of cooperation and on another for the development of conflict. From some viewpoints, it appears probable that conflict is least likely to occur over the allocation of scarce goods, for the allocation of scarce goods without conflict is considered a principal function of society. Surely it is simpler to consider a conflict to exist when people say that it exists—namely, when two or more individuals act toward each other in a way recognized by other members of the society as showing conflict. This may or may not involve scarce goods, as the case may be. It is worth noting that Simmel (1955, p. 27) never accepted the notion that conflict inevitably occurs over scarce goods:

If the conflict is caused by an object, by the will to have or control something, by rage or revenge, such a desired object or state of affairs make for conditions which subject the fight to norms or restrictions applying to both warring parties. Moreover, since the fight is centered in a purpose outside itself, it is qualified by the fact that, in principle, every end can be attained by more than one means. The desire for possession or subjugation, even for the annihilation of the enemy, can be satisfied through combinations and events other than fight.

Finally, although the folklore of upper classes sometimes attributes vast and uncontrolled aggressive impulses to lower classes, it must be admitted that over most of the world the dispossessed are not noted for violence or conflict.

But there are other possible reasons for conflict. Perhaps there may be an error in receiving or transmitting symbols. The Namhalli neighbor *may* have been attempting to help out when she swept in front of the other woman's house, or she may have thought she was sweeping her own section of the street. The two neighbors may have had different cultural backgrounds: perhaps the neighbor had just moved to the village from the city, and no one had told her that cow dung was not fair game as it is in the city. And at Taos, the conflict over water—a scarce good—may have come about from a mistake in interpreting the irrigation schedule. This same sort of error in the perception of external events may also have taken place at Namhalli. Just who has rights over cow dung lying on the property line between two houses? In both the Namhalli and Taos examples, scarce, or at least desirable, goods are involved in the conflict. Thus, even when conflict appears to arise solely from an attempt to force conformity to social regulations, it can be argued that the basic motive is anxiety arising from scarcity. But here again we come back to our argument, for surely no man would do anything unless he felt that it would improve his condition in one way or another. The circle can be made complete by suggesting that the only sure way of knowing that desire (and therefore scarcity) exists is by observing the movement of the organism. If scarce goods are the basis of conflict and the cause of all human activity as well, it follows that the purpose of all human activity is to engage in conflict—indeed a sorry picture. A classification of conflict in terms of scarce goods may be useful under certain circumstances, but not to those who are concerned with the activity of organizations or cultural systems. What would seem to be important from such a standpoint is the nature of the activity, an exchange of oppositions, and the effect of that activity on the organization.

KINDS OF CONFLICT

Any definition of conflict based on how an exchange of oppositions affects an organization must acknowledge that the organization can be affected in two ways: subjectively and objectively. If people *think* that there is so much conflict that nothing can be done, the effect is almost the same as if there actually is so much conflict that nothing can be done. Both kinds of effect are usually found to occur simultaneously. Where they do not, a state of confusion is implied, and it may be supposed that the more disruptive form of conflict is present. Conflict can be classified in terms of the extent to which the normal operation of the organization is interrupted. This is the criterion of disruption. It is paralleled in the area of meaning by the interpretation of the conflict as beneficial or detrimental by members of the society. Conflict that is nondisruptive and is regarded as beneficial is perhaps best termed pseudoconflict.

When exchanges of oppositions reach a point where they make impossible the carrying out of routine tasks, it may be expected that there will be systematic attempts to bring the divisive conflict to a halt. Where conflict is amenable to normal processes of arbitration, it remains relatively nondisruptive. Members of the group may regard such conflict as detrimental, but it will not create surprise or dismay. Such conflict may be described as normal dispute.

Where regulation of conflict becomes difficult or impossible, there will be a consequent disruption of activities that will be equally difficult or impossible to remedy. This sort of conflict will be considered unusual and unexpected. Such a state of affairs, presumably neither as widely distributed nor as frequent as normal dispute, can be described as factionalist dispute.

Using the criterion of disruption, then, it is possible to distinguish major points of difference between pseudoconflict and divisive conflict and between normal dispute and factionalist dispute. Factionalist dispute, regardless of whether it is *caused* by organizational change, is the only variety of conflict that necessarily involves major organizational changes. Another important criterion is the extent to which conflict is between individuals or between organized groups. An organization in which nobody is capable of getting along with anyone else is disrupted quite as much as an organization in which two well-organized groups engage in continuous and unregulated conflict. We have, then, a threshold below which conflict is not of *organizational* significance, although it may be significant to subdivisions of the organization. Beyond that it is possible to speak of tendencies toward individualistic conflict and toward organized conflict or schism. Here, there is no clear difference between the two varieties of conflict, for it is impossible to speak realistically of perfect individualistic conflict or of perfect dualistic organization. Pseudoconflict can be divided into individual competition and team play; normal dispute can be divided into argument and party conflict; factionalist dispute can be divided into pervasive factionalism and schismatic factionalism (see Fig. 1). In real life, the forms of individualistic conflict appear to involve temporary alliances and group formations of the type some authors would describe as factions. Groups of this type differ from teams, parties, or schismatic factions in that they tend to persist only for the purposes of a particular conflict, whereas parties change membership relatively slowly. It appears probable that there can be horizontal shifts from individualistic to group conflict, or from group to individualistic conflict, without there being any noticeable increase in the degree of conflict.

FIG. 1—VARIETIES OF CONFLICT

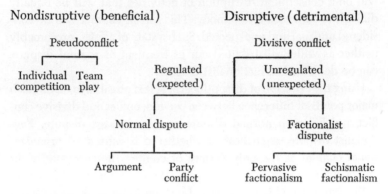

In addition to the criterion of disruption and the extent to which it involves organized groups, conflict can be described in terms of the levels at which it occurs within the organization. Turner (1957, p. 91) remarks:

On a number of occasions during my fieldwork I became aware of marked disturbance in the social life of the particular group I happened to be studying at the time. The whole group might be radically cloven into two conflicting factions; the quarreling parties might comprise some but not all of its members, or disputes might be merely interpersonal in character. Disturbance in short had a variable range of social inclusiveness.

As Turner goes on to say, conflict may be sealed off within some segment of an organization, or it may develop until all or most of the membership is involved. This type of escalation might be described as escalation in scope rather than in severity. The War of Jenkins' Ear, had it really been fought over Jenkins' ear, would suggest the type of escalation involved. In the same way, in Namhalli a quarrel between housewives could conceivably become a matter serious enough to disrupt village affairs. Turner traces an escalation from "breach" through "mounting crisis" to the application of adjustive and redressive mechanisms, and on to a final phase in which the matter is either resolved or not. Actually, redressive mechanisms are brought into play at every stage as escalation in scope occurs. When escalation in scope exhausts all existing organizational levels (where the emperor himself cannot stop the conflict), Turner's "irreparable breach" occurs and the organization dissolves. In classifying conflict types, then, we may, if absolutely necessary, distinguish among conflicts at the familial, neighborhood, tribal, national, or international levels. When an organization exists at many levels of integration, conflict may be restrained simply by the length of time and the amount of effort required to escalate the conflict across the levels. The Ndembu and the Pueblo Indians, for example, face actual fission far more frequently than such villages as Namhalli, which can, as a last resort, appeal to larger organizations.

It is possible that the distinction made here between normal dispute and factionalist dispute is approximately the same as the distinction normally made between functional and dysfunctional conflict. Where conflict, no matter how disruptive, is subject to regulatory devices that force a return to normal group functioning, it is likely to acquire an organized and ritualistic character. Whether or not this is to be regarded as functional depends very much upon one's definition of function. If "What is, is right," then conflict that follows a well-defined and predictable course is unquestionably fixed into the structure of the organization. Abandonment of such "normal" conflict would create major changes. It can thus be said that the conflict is essential for the preservation of the organization as it is. So far, there appear to be no writers willing to explain whether or not conflict contributes to food production or reproduction and if so in what way.

Some authors (LeVine, 1961, pp. 3–4, for example) see important differences between our views and the views of such writers as Coser, Gluckman, Turner, and Simmel, in terms of whether or not they view conflict as eufunctional or dysfunctional. Coser (1957, p. 205) remarks: "If the tensions that need outlets are continually reproduced within the structure, abreaction through tensions release mechanisms may preserve the system but at the risk of ever-renewed further accumulation of tension. Such accumulation eventuates easily in the eruption of destructive unrealistic conflict." Possibly Coser feels that even "destructive unrealistic conflicts" are functional, and indeed every cloud has a silver lining. Turner writes of "irreparable breach" as functional for Ndembu society as a whole (1957, p. 91), but one wonders if he regards it as functional for the community that is breached. Presumably an atomic war on Earth would be functional for Martians. If we use the term "function" to mean simply desirable or undesirable, there is always some point of view from which a conflict is desirable. Either conflict leads to change or it doesn't. If it does lead to change, that is obviously functional; if it doesn't lead to change, that is obviously functional as well. What has been gained by describing conflict as functional? If conflict is described in terms of such concepts as breach, disruption, and regulation, it is possible to describe exactly what has been breached, disrupted, or regulated. Any given conflict has functional and dysfunctional aspects; nothing is gained by debating whether or not conflict in the abstract is functional.

One final point that can be made concerning divisiveness is implied by the term itself. Divisiveness differs from warfare between distinct groups in that divisiveness always carries with it the threat that a valued organization will suffer—to use Turner's words—an irreparable breach. Simmel (1955, p. 48–49) says:

[Social hatred] is directed against a member of the group, not from personal motives, but because the member represents a danger to the preservation of the group. Insofar as intragroup conflict involves such a danger, the two conflicting parties hate each other not only on the concrete ground which produced the conflict but also on the sociological ground of hatred for the enemy of the group itself. Since this hatred is mutual and each accuses the other of responsibility for the threat to the whole, the antagonism sharpens—precisely because both parties to it belong to the same social unit.

In other words, where there is divisiveness, the goal of maintaining the organization is always in evidence. Fission (the irreparable breach), secession, or disbandment reflect the giving up of organizational goals, and may or may not involve conflict. This point is also relevant to conflicts that occur when representatives of different organizations are brought into continual relationship, when nations are arbitrarily created by colonial powers, or when different tribes or bands of Indians are confined to the same reservation (see Clifton, 1963). Divisiveness implies the presence of divisions within an established unit, not the establishment of a divided unit. Clifton and others have seen dramatic similarities between the artificial communities of Indian reservations and established communities such as Taos and Namhalli, but it remains necessary to explore further such problems as the extent to which expressed oppositions are meaningful in artificial communities and the extent to which it is possible to speak of common goals. Insofar as reservation communities represent a transition from the artificial to the natural community, one might expect an inverse movement from war to feud to party conflict.

CONCLUSION

LeVine (1961, p. 5) is typical of the group of modern writers who suggest that the causes of conflict are, at least in part, to be found in animal behavior: "What are the causes of conflict in human social systems? Whatever they are, it is safe to assume that not all of them are peculiar to *homo sapiens*, since aggressive behavior is found widely among the vertebrates and is presumably adaptive in a broad range of environments." It is our opinion that since animals do not talk, they are unable to develop complex symbolic systems and to indulge in the meaningful exchange of oppositions that we call conflict dialogue. Aggression is a psychological motive that can be understood as aggression only when properly interpreted. Human individuals may express opposition to other individuals for a variety of motives, of which aggression is only one. We agree with Simmel (1955, p. 33):

No matter how much psychological autonomy one may be willing to grant the antagonistic drive, this autonomy is not enough to account for all phenomena involving hostility. . . . On the other hand, it seems probable to me that on the whole, because of its formal character, the hostility drive merely adds itself as a reinforcement (like the pedal on the piano, as it were) to controversies which are due to concrete causes.

In our search for possible causes of the initiation and prolongation of conflict dialogues, we have not found it necessary to call up Contentious Man, Economic Man, Libidinous Man, Frustrated Man, or any others. With Lewis Carroll, we accept the general notion that a fish never goes any place without a porpoise, and refuse to speculate upon its nature. With Turner (1957, p. 91), Nader and Metzger (1963, p. 589), and Kopytoff (1961, p. 65), we are of the opinion that conflict should be described in terms of breaches of normally expected behavior that lead to a dialogue recognized as an exchange of oppositions. The data we have accumulated so far appears to be amenable to a social and cultural analysis rather than to a biological or physiological analysis. Perhaps other definitions will prove empirically useful for other purposes.

We have distinguished a number of types of conflict, including pseudoconflict, divisive conflict, normal dispute, and factionalist dispute. We have divided normal dispute into argument and party conflict, and we have divided factionalist dispute into pervasive factionalism and schismatic factionalism. The fact that it is possible to make such distinctions tells us little about the firmness of the lines separating the different types. The borderline between pseudoconflict and conflict often depends upon one's point of view: at a football match some spectators may think that the opposing team is displaying excessive roughness. For them, a state of conflict may be said to exist. As more and more spectators come to feel that such a state exists, the signs of opposition between the partisans of the two teams are likely to become less and less playful to the point where authorities feel that action must be taken. Even at this point the conflict may be regarded as nothing more than one of those things that sometimes happen at football games. When the spectators themselves come to blows or the game is disrupted, obviously it is reasonable to say that a state of conflict exists. In the same way, it is difficult to draw a line between some kinds of electioneering and revolution. Election day riots may be perfectly normal and arouse little comment, or they may be regarded as a national disaster. In dividing conflict into types, our attention has been directed toward those points at which increases in scale (the degree of threatened disruption), scope (the size of the social unit involved), and pervasiveness (the number of kinds of relationships disrupted along a scale ranging from total individualistic conflict to schism) might be expected to produce marked differences in behavior.

Such points, at which escalation calls for changes in behavior, must be identified in terms of the system of meanings existing in each organization. In Taos virtually any exchange of overt opposition is likely to be interpreted as a dispute calling for immediate intervention. In Namhalli intervention in conflicts between women, even when they become violent, is rare, whereas conflicts between men or between men and women are usually interrupted as soon as there is physical violence, or the threat of violence. In both communities skilled leaders may intervene long before the conflict has grown to the point that it attracts attention. The precise definition of types and stages of conflict requires a careful analysis of the successive meanings attributed to the conflict as it develops and of its effects on organizational membership and functioning.

Our study is intended to illustrate by reference to Taos and Namhalli some of the major aspects of conflict. We do not undertake to explore all of the varieties defined here—not from lack of desire, but from lack of information. A thorough discussion of conflict requires a knowledge of preexisting social arrangements, of the conditions that led to the emergence of the conflict, and of the stages through which the conflict has passed. No detailed descriptions of these stages exist in the literature. Turner's work on the Ndembu is the most complete discussion, yet it has little to say about cultural change. Thus we are limited to a discussion of factionalist dispute at Taos and Namhalli. Chapters 2–4 will deal with those stable or structural characteristics of both communities that appear to have led to a tendency toward functionalist dispute. Chapter 5 will discuss certain patterns of stress, or change in the total surroundings, that appear to have encouraged the development of factionalist dispute. Chapters 6 and 7 will describe the resulting conflicts in the two villages, and Chapter 8 will attempt to arrive at theoretical understandings.

2. The Background of Conflict in Namhalli

If conflict is an exchange of behaviors symbolizing opposition, then the possibility of conflict and the nature of conflict are profoundly influenced by the system of meanings provided in the cultural tradition. The choice of conflict behavior from among the alternatives available suggests that in some way conflict behavior promises to both parties a surer method of achieving goals than do other behaviors. Logically it is difficult to imagine why two parties would simultaneously choose to oppose each other except when they have equal chances of winning. When the odds are unequal, it follows that at least one party is either sufficiently desperate or sufficiently misinformed to be willing to accept unfavorable odds. Even in the case where a conflict is begun with a view to securing the interven· tion of a third party, it appears likely that such intervention is always more costly than voluntary settlement of a disagreement before the stage of open conflict or intervention is reached.

Where conflict can be traced to a failure to predict the outcome of a particular situation, the origins of conflict may be found in those aspects of the cultural tradition and its setting that lead to failures of prediction or of perception. Such failures and misinterpretations can occur in the problem solutions used by the organization in coping with its environment, and they can exist in terms of contradictions and inconsistencies within the cultural tradition. Consideration of the background of conflict in Namhalli may well begin with a discussion of the set of problems or external conditions that have more or less continuously affected the village.

EXTERNAL CONDITIONS

Within the larger regional and urban culture to which it belongs, Namhalli's principal role is to produce agricultural commodities demanded by urban populations and by military, political, and religious establishments designed to secure the boundaries of the larger society. As a part-society, a village must conform to the general cultural pattern of the villages surrounding it, so as to be, in important ways, a replicate of its neighbors. For this reason, a village rarely develops independent solutions to problems, but tends to utilize regionally available solutions. The maintenance of conformity to a regional culture cannot be allowed to jeopardize the village's basic functions of exporting agricultural produce and maintaining its own population. Namhalli, then, can be regarded as the product of compromises between ecological necessities and the demands of the regional culture. Because the delicate balance between ecological and sociological imperatives is maintained through decisions made within the village, it is possible to regard the cultural tradition of Namhalli *as if* it had been devised on the spot for the purpose of dealing with the problems of the membership of the village. Some of those problems, defined as external conditions, are described below.

In early days, the site of Namhalli was a forested plain sloping gently downward toward a small stream that formed the eastern boundary of the village territory. The soil was a characteristic mixture of red clay and sand, which, although not infertile, may have been somewhat lacking in organic matter. Such a soil does not absorb moisture rapidly and heavy rains can cause considerable run-off. Wild life was not abundant, but it included tigers, leopards, deer, boar, and probably elephants. The forest was not so dense as to make the clearing of land difficult. The climate was mild, and rainfall was moderate but with considerable annual variation.

Low hills, outcroppings of granite, and the forested countryside were sufficient to make communication difficult and continuous

political control of the region almost impossible. The first settlers
of Namhalli and those who subsequently resettled it at various
periods had, then, to adjust to a politically unstable region. Because Namhalli is newer than some of the surrounding villages,
adjustments and concessions had to be made to nearby established
communities. Throughout the history of Mysore State, the Namhalli region has been part of larger kingdoms and states. Mostly
government has been in the hands of local chieftains who emerged
periodically from their fortifications to collect taxes. Such chieftains had slight interest in the maintenance of law and order, and
were often incapable of protecting the villages under their jurisdic-
tion from cattle thieves and bandits. Local epigraphic and mytho-
logic sources do not, in any case, make strong distinctions between
bandits and chieftains. Somewhat independent of the military-
political machinery was an elaborate regional religious hierarchy
whose major function was to maintain good relationships between
the people of the region and a complex hierarchy of deities. Another, somewhat less sociological, type of problem posed by external conditions was the periodic appearance of such diseases as
smallpox, cholera, and, later, bubonic plague. This was balanced
by a relatively low incidence of endemic diseases and a climate
that tourist pamphlets describe as healthful.

These specific external conditions, together with relatively universal conditions such as needs for companionship, sex, play, exploration, social control, and enculturation, posed certain problems
for the community. There had to be enough surplus (over what
the community members needed) to cover the payment of taxes,
the meeting of religious obligations, the maintenance of trade relationships with neighboring villages, and the storage of food
against the event of crop failure. The community also had to maintain an immigration rate and birthrate high enough to offset losses
due to mortality and emigration, but not so high as to overtax productive resources. Friendly relationships with neighboring communities had to be maintained for purposes of protection and exchange, and the community had to be organized against human
and animal marauders. The cultural tradition of Namhalli contains

solutions to these particular problems and to the more general problems encountered by all or most human communities. Because not only survival but also such things as esthetic satisfaction are at stake, the solution provided must be elegant—it must solve all problems at once and as consistently as possible.

DIRECT COPING

Many community problems can be handled or even erased in a direct and technical manner. But technical solutions can lead to the development of secondary problems, and these, along with the primary problems posed by external conditions (including the nature of man), constitute the over-all set of problems facing a community. Technical solutions to the problem of food production were evidently available at the time Namhalli was established, the broad pattern of subsistence being characteristic of the region. Basically this was plow agriculture, in which bullocks were used to draw the plow and substantial herds of cattle and sheep provided manure. Manuring, composting, and intercropping with leguminous plants made it possible to raise crops on the same land over prolonged periods. The principal crop, finger millet (*Eleusine corocana*), tolerates a relatively poor soil and a wide range of moisture conditions. It is grown in association with legumes, oil seeds, and fodder crops, so that the crop grown in a single field provides an almost complete diet for men and animals.

Compared with rice or sorghum, finger millet does not produce a very heavy yield per acre. Like most grain crops, finger millet has strong seasonal variation in its labor requirements. A five-acre field of millet and associated crops normally requires the full-time labor of a nuclear family over a six-month period, with additional labor for planting, weeding, transplanting, and harvesting. If the field is to produce enough to meet such external commitments as taxation and religious dues, the farmer must find some way to obtain seasonal labor at low cost.

Minor agricultural activities included trapping run-off water in ponds and using the water for such short-season irrigated crops as chilies and eggplant. Moist lands near the stream were used for orchard or garden crops. Uncultivated lands were used for grazing goats, sheep, and cattle. The various agricultural techniques appeared to have produced enough to serve the needs of the village during good or average years, but not to meet the famine conditions likely to occur every twenty or thirty years.

Problems of defense were handled technically by guarding fields during the growing season and fencing gardens with thorny shrubs. Residents and cattle lived close together in the center of the village lands, protected by a hedge of thorns and by deep pits filled with water. This kind of direct coping was sufficiently effective to meet the major problems posed by external conditions, except for organized armed attack, disease, and famine.

The techniques of directly coping with external conditions outlined above have permitted the survival of the village of Namhalli over a considerable period of time. In general the problem solutions provided have not been perfect, and the relationships between Namhalli and the world around it have never been completely stable or predictable. The farmer, when he plants his crop, is reasonably certain of an adequate harvest, but the exact amount of the harvest is unpredictable. In 1877 and 1966 crop failure was almost total. Bandits never succeeded in wiping out the village, nor did government tax collectors ever discover all the reserves of grain hidden in pits under the streets or in the fields. Nevertheless, these possibilities were never completely excluded by the various devices designed to cope with the external environment.

Even had Namhalli's techniques of direct coping solved all problems posed by external conditions as completely as possible, there still would have remained the problems created by the techniques themselves—secondary problems arise from the application of problem-solving devices. In Namhalli, the solution of subsistence and production problems by agriculture leads to the problem of obtaining cheap seasonal labor. The wide range of types of agriculture creates the problem of arranging a firm division of labor even within the family. If holdings are of moderate size, one man is required to herd cattle, one man to raise millet crops, and one man to supervise the garden. Because agriculture requires specialized tools, there must be specialists to make them. Because grain crops can be grown only at certain seasons, there must be storage facilities. The defense of Namhalli against marauders spawned by unsettled political conditions involved the development of a strongly centralized village organization integrally connected to a regional political and social structure.

Such tasks as finding cheap labor or prevailing upon one's younger brother to supervise the family garden do not represent direct solutions of problems posed by external conditions. Problems originating at the level of external conditions have repercussions at the ideological and sociological levels. These repercussions are problems in their own right, but they must often be handled by means of indirect techniques.

INDIRECT COPING

Techniques of indirect coping deal with problems by ideological or sociological means. Indirect coping involves changing the way the membership thinks or changing the relationships among the members, but it does not involve any direct attack upon the external problem confronting the organization. In the case of Namhalli, ideological coping is of particular importance where direct coping fails. The key doctrine providing an explanation for such failure is the belief, drawn from the wider Indian system of beliefs, that the phenomenal world is not reality. Crop failure, illness, and all other misfortunes encountered in the everyday world can be met by the statement "Things are not what they seem." The pain of failure and misfortune derives from the fact that one has become unduly concerned with the phenomenal world. Freedom from the sorrows and misfortunes of this world is readily available to anyone prepared to follow appropriate formulae to achieve understanding of the ultimate reality.

Such a belief cannot stand alone as the basis for a cultural tradition, since it involves no incentive for activity within the phenomenal world. The first great inconsistency in Namhalli's belief system is the argument that the search for ultimate reality must be limited to those who are capable of ignoring their own sense im-

pressions. Such persons are those who with their eyes open see
nothing, who have ears but hear nothing, who feel neither pain,
nor hunger, nor grief at the loss of loved ones. Such persons are
believed to be extremely rare, and those who claim such abilities
are usually considered to be fraudulent. Old men or persons who
have been deprived of their responsibilities to others by misfortune
may legitimately attempt, through austerities and an abandonment
of worldly concerns, to achieve the status of "saint." But since ordinary persons are considered responsible for the training and spiritual development of persons under their care, it is impossible for
them to act like saints, no matter how saintly their nature may be.
To abandon one's wife, children, and other dependents in order to
save oneself is regarded as cowardly. From considerations of this
kind arises the concept of levels of spiritual development.

Rebirth and fate

Every person leads a series of lives in the phenomenal world. He
continues to be born and reborn until he achieves the capacity to
free himself from the illusion that the phenomenal world is real.
Most people have not yet achieved that capacity, and therefore
the average person must come to terms with the phenomenal world
and try to devote each lifetime to achieving as much independence
as he can from the illusion of life. During any one lifetime, the goal
is not to achieve freedom from the phenomenal world, but to
achieve sufficient spiritual growth so that in some future lifetime
he will be in a position to achieve freedom. The twin goals of
achieving freedom and of participating in the phenomenal world
may seem inconsistent, but the theory of levels of development
provides a defense against recognition of the inconsistency. Most
men are not sufficiently advanced to be capable of fully understanding the traditional explanations of the belief system. The citizen of Namhalli believes that the explanations are consistent and
logical, and that persons exist who are wise enough to explain it all.

The ultimate law of the universe is *dharma*. In one sense everything that happens is in accordance with dharma, the perfect functioning of the universe. If a man could carry out his existence in

perfect conformity with dharma, in the slightly different sense of absolute righteousness, he would be assured of achieving ultimate release from worldly cares. The average person cannot conform to dharma because he lacks sufficient spiritual advancement to be capable of understanding what dharma is. The average person *does* possess access to the laws of *karma,* which govern the behavior of a person at his own particular level of development. Because all actions ultimately conform to dharma, a man may achieve spiritual promotion either through conformity to the laws of karma (proper execution of his role in life) or through conformity to the laws of dharma (doing the right thing no matter what). This choice means that in the phenomenal world there are multiple ethics connected with all possible actions. There is a conflict not only between laws of dharma and karma, but also between different kinds of karma. Each social role specifies its own karma or duty, and each man plays many roles. The concept of levels of spiritual development (necessary to provide an ethical basis for action within the context of a belief system that rejects the phenomenal world as unreal) leads inevitably and logically to a multiple morality, in which persons playing one social role are required to utilize a set of values different from that of those playing another social role.

The taking of life, for example, is a violation of dharma; it is sinful in the sense of ultimate morality. Many persons are born into groups at such a low level of spiritual development that they are incapable of understanding this basic moral principle. Were those who took the lives of sheep, goats, or cattle regarded as committing sins when they did so, the prospects for persons of low rank would indeed be grim, for they would be denied any possibility of spiritual development. In fact, such persons are considered to be virtuous despite the fact that they take life. They are fulfilling their proper role. A born meat eater may improve his position in future rebirths *either* by refusing to eat meat (dharma) or by continuing to eat meat (karma). There are "many roads to heaven," and every man is offered a wide variety of methods that he can use to achieve a more favorable rebirth or perhaps freedom from the phenomenal world.

Because each person's sins and virtues are weighed at the time of his death, and are used to determine what will happen to him in his next life, a man must accept the circumstances of his birth. The fact that he is born into a low or high place has no effect on his capacity to perform good or evil actions. A king or a father may be good or evil. If he is evil, he can expect to be reborn in a low position. Similarly, a subject or a son may be either good or evil. If he is good, he may look forward to a favorable rebirth. The concept of rebirth, then, admits a kind of spiritual equality within the notion of an inequality of hereditary positions: the good servant has better prospects than the bad master. In a sense, equality and dharma are long-term spiritual concepts; inequality and karma are short-term, worldly concepts.

The Age of Kali

In a well-run universe, one might expect that even the phenomenal world would be predictable and orderly. This is believed to be true except for periods when there is an appearance of disorder. The present age, the Age of Kali, is such a period. Because the phenomenal world is currently being run by a woman, the goddess Kali, it is subject to misgovernment. Virtue sometimes appears to be unrewarded, and evil men sometimes gain access to high positions. If every person acted in absolute conformity to karma and dharma, such things as crop failure would not occur, rains would be predictable and in appropriate quantities, and everything that happened would follow a normal and predictable course in accordance with the ideal patterns laid down in the cultural tradition. During the Age of Kali, kings and rulers are weak. There is a great deal of sin and a great deal of divine punishment.

Divine punishment may be part of the fate written upon each man's forehead by the supreme deity, Brahma, or it may be direct punishment for sins committed in this life. Such punishments are administered by female goddesses, evidently forms of the goddess Kali, or, more rarely, by witches or evil spirits. Divine reward can come about in many more ways. Intense worship of a single deity; absolute conformity to a particular ethical code; any kind of sacrifice; performance of magical rites having compelling force; or uttering one of the names of God upon one's deathbed—all these may result in reward. Whenever a man encounters an unpredicted event construed as either rewarding or punishing, it can be attributed to the virtues or vices of the individual or his close associates. Misfortunes that fall on an obviously virtuous man are explained as a "test," or as punishment for sins committed in a previous life or for sins committed by his wife or children. Sometimes the gods will punish a family or an entire village by removing a valued member. Any misfortune, either individual or collective, leads to the question of who sinned and whose behavior must be altered in order to remove the threat of further punishment.

If misfortunes, particularly such collective misfortunes as famine and disease, are to be attributed to sinful behavior within the community, it follows that the community must be able to identify and control those likely to commit sins. There is a need in the community for persons who not only are familiar with the nature of sinful behavior but are in a position to prevent its occurrence— in other words, persons who carried out their previous lives in a virtuous manner and were rewarded by being placed, through birth, in favorable social roles. Brahmins, Jangamas, and others born to command are expected to instruct their subordinates concerning virtuous behavior and to apply punishment where necessary.

Because different varieties of virtuous behavior are applicable to each social role, and because each individual plays several roles, the definition of proper and improper behavior is not easy. Written precedents in the form of laws, charters, and religious texts and tales represent attempts to specify proper behaviors in a wide variety of contexts. Problems arise when unprecedented situations occur or where a person occupies two statuses having conflicting obligations. A younger brother has responsibilities toward his wife and toward his elder brother. Ordinarily, carrying out such responsibilities could not involve any indecision, but because this is the Age of Kali, the behavior of wives and elder brothers is unpredictable, and the younger brother is all too often placed in an awkward position. The village drama traditionally performed in Namhalli is the story of the famous gambling game in which the eldest of the Pandava brothers, Dharmarayya, loses the communal wife, Draupadi, to his wicked cousins in a crooked contest. The other Pandava brothers wish to declare war upon the wicked cousins, but the eldest brother, knowing what is right (dharma) as always, insists that the obligation must be honored. The younger brothers threaten to repudiate the eldest brother, but finally give in, sacrificing wife for brother.

Situations of this kind arise from the inconsistencies of karma and dharma, and from the distinctions made between the phenomenal world and the world of ultimate reality. The religious tale advocating the importance of fraternal loyalty over obligations to wives is an attempt to shore up the system of social relationships at a point where it is weak. In real life the system is supported by strongly punitive authority capable of determining which of two choices is appropriate and of enforcing conformity to the appropriate choice.

THE VILLAGE ORDER

The ideal structure of the village is a set of castes (*jatis*) arranged in a hierarchy. Each caste owes particular obligations to every other caste, and each caste performs essential complementary services for every other caste. These obligations and services are in each case part of the karma of the caste. Members acquire spiritual advancement by performing their traditional functions. Authority is vested in the highest-ranking castes, which are charged with the duties of instructing and disciplining those of lower rank. Analogous relationships are those of father and son, master and servant, lender and borrower, elder brother and younger brother, elder wife (or husband's elder brother's wife) and younger wife, mother-in-law and daughter-in-law, father and daughter, mother and daughter, and brother and sister. The principles that generate these relationships are: (1) pure castes are higher than impure castes, (2) men are higher than women, (3) rich people are higher than poor people, and (4) older people are

higher than younger people. These principles are not mutually exclusive; it is the fact that they overlap within particular social
relationships that causes strain.

In theory, such overlapping cannot occur, and disagreements
cannot arise concerning the responsibilities of one person toward
another. In practice, the Age of Kali and the existence of conflicting
interpretations of dharma and karma create considerable confusion. The ranking of castes, for example, is not clearly established.
Among the highest-ranking pure vegetarian castes in Namhalli, the
Brahmins, the Lingayats, and the Pancalas (artisans) all claim to
be of the highest rank. Such disagreement may be a result of the
fact that there has never been a strong permanent regional authority capable of legislating a definite hierarchy of castes, or it may
stem from the kind of factor discussed by McKim Marriott (1960).

In times past, Namhalli possessed a relatively strong authority
structure so that a definite hierarchy of castes was maintained at
the behavioral level if not at the ideological level. The leaders of
the village, its "mother and father," were the Accountant chosen
from the Brahmin caste and the Headman chosen from the Jangama caste. Because the village had originally been established
by a Jangama, the Headman was the dominant figure. Later, actual
leadership shifted to a cabal of important men who cooperated
with the Headman.

At the level of meat-eating castes, Weavers and Shepherds
claimed to be of equal status, but Weavers tended to be given
slightly greater recognition in village councils. Muslims, also claiming to be superior to all other castes on an ideological basis, accepted a position slightly below that of the Shepherds. The Madigas (leatherworkers and laborers) were the lowest-ranking caste
in the village, but they were considerably better off economically
than the members of such minor castes as Basketweaver and Hunter. The presence of particular castes in a village has to do with the
net reproductive rates of particular families, and with the interaction between environmental factors and traditional caste occupations. The presence and size of the Weaver, Shepherd, and
Madiga castes, insofar as they followed their traditional occupa-

tions, appears to have been the result of economic circumstances beyond the control of the village organization. Had Namhalli specialized in rice production it probably would have had greater need for laborers and so for more Madigas; had the village grazing lands been smaller, it probably would have had fewer Shepherds. In other words, because each village faces a different set of external conditions, and solves them in a somewhat different way, each village has a unique caste structure. The ideology of caste hierarchy is less variable and acquires regional, if not pan-Indian, significance. In effect, each village must constitute itself in response to its particular situation, and since situations differ, some villages will find it more difficult than others to develop a suitable caste hierarchy in conformity to regionally accepted ideals. Where there are such difficulties, individual castes are likely to enter into conflict concerning their place in the structure.

These problems were dealt with, at one level, by village authorities, mainly by the Headman. On a more subtle level, the doctrine of the interdependency of all castes, together with the requirement of multicaste participation in all important ceremonial and economic activities, served to lessen intercaste strains and conflicts. A marriage, for example, had to be approved by representatives of virtually every caste. Major calendrical ceremonies also required multiple participation. An aggrieved individual or group could practice or threaten to practice a boycott, and thus ensure discussion and adjudication of the grievance. Another aspect of caste interdependence was the formation of the village council on the basis of equal representation from each of the major castes. Because agreement on council decisions had to be unanimous, intercaste disputes would have paralyzed the council. Both the doctrine of caste interdependence and the practice of equal representation reflect the fundamental conflict between the principles of hierarchy and equality.

Caste conflict was also controlled within Namhalli by the fact that there were five or six, rather than one or two, numerically large castes, which meant that in a dispute between any two castes, most other castes, having nothing to gain, would tend to mediate rather than take sides. Since the Madiga, the lowest-ranking caste, represented only about one-fifth of the total population, the possibilities of "class war" were correspondingly limited. Still another barrier to intercaste conflict was the extension of caste ties by means of marriage between villages. Conflict between castes in one village would tend to have regional repercussions, perhaps in villages where the balance of power between the two opposed castes was quite different. In the village where the conflict started relatives and moneylenders from other villages would begin applying economic and social pressures designed to control the conflict. In the case of Namhalli, the small size of the village may also have tended to suppress intercaste conflict, since there were relatively few alternative sources of goods and services. Since all of the castes in Namhalli consisted of a few families each, groups of age-mates inevitably were drawn from all castes, excluding only the Madiga. In the event of intercaste conflict, the degree of disruption of social life would have been proportionately greater than in a large village composed of large castes tending to form exclusive groups.

THE YAJAMAN

Traditionally each of the castes in Namhalli was composed of one or two large families, and related nuclear families consisting of widows, relatives by marriage, or separated brothers with their families. The head of one of the large families was the head of his caste and its representative on the village council and on the regional caste council. Within the caste, then, there was a single dominant authority or headman (*yajaman*). Succession to the position of family and caste headman was determined by lineage membership, age, and ability to perform the traditional duties in an acceptable manner. Theoretically, the family, lineage, or caste headman retired when he became too old or when he became incompetent to perform his duties for any reason. Where the criteria of age and competence were in dispute, as in the case of an incompetent older man, conflict was frequent and had to be dealt with by higher authorities like the village Headman, government

officials, or religious officials. In addition to the position of headman, caste and lineage membership often carried with it particular
responsibilities and prerogatives. A particular group might have
the right to provide a priest for a particular temple, to perform
some particular economic function, or to plow certain lands. Competing lineages within the same caste, or competing branches of
the same lineage, might well enter into conflict over succession
to such positions, notably when the rightful heir was underage or
where there was no male child to inherit.

Another yajaman, the family head, was expected to be obeyed
by all without question. The authority of the family head was
parallel to the authority of mother-in-law over daughter-in-law,
elder brother over younger brother, husband over wife, and elder
wife over younger wife. Despite the apparent rigidity and strength
of such a family hierarchy of age and sex, it had a compensating
mechanism—the common ownership of property by the male members of the family. At any time, a son or younger brother could insist upon his rights and withdraw from the joint family. A daughter-
in-law could prevail upon her husband to withdraw or could flee
to her parents' house.

In the perfect family, five brothers are supposed to divide the
labor, one taking charge of family finances and marketing, another
farming the millet fields, a third caring for the cattle, a fourth managing the garden, and a fifth carrying out the family trade or occupation. The division was not equal, but each brother was supposed to operate more or less autonomously within his own sphere.
Unless the population is increasing rapidly, relatively few families
can consist of five brothers. All too often the joint family, containing three generations under one roof, must have consisted of five
or six people rather than the ideal fifty or one hundred. Lacking
an ideal joint family, most people had no clear model for the division of labor, profits, and property within their own seemingly
atypical family.

Possibly due to the fact that most families did not fit the ideal
model, family headmen were expected to exercise almost super-
human restraint in their dealings with subordinates. Dharmarayya,

the eldest of the five perfect Pandava brothers and the patron saint of the city of Bangalore, was, as his name suggests, mainly noted for his fanatical adherence to morality and perfect fairness. Where the family headman seemed not to be adhering to dharma, the subordinate was ideally required to voice his protests in indirect ways, avoiding any direct opposition to the headman. Prolonged complaint and argument were apparently not regarded as direct disobedience or even as disrespectful. Where prolonged complaint failed to bring an easing of the troubles, the injured subordinate was supposed to withdraw by working inefficiently, refusing to eat, sulking, retreating to the garden house and weeping, or, if all else failed, jumping into a well. Ordinarily, an underfed or distraught appearance was sufficient to provoke intervention and mediation of family conflict.

The village Headman, the caste headman, and the family headman—in fact all persons bearing the title of yajaman—faced practically identical problems and had almost identical relationships with their subordinates (see Table 1). This means that strains in the family are parallel to strains in the caste and in the village.

Husband and wife

The husband-wife relationship presents several particular problems not summarized in Table 1. Marriages are usually arranged, often for the purpose of establishing friendly relationships between families and between villages. The unavailability of suitable brides within the village and the desire to promote intervillage relationships has lead to a situation in which approximately two-thirds of the wives in Namhalli were born in other villages. This degree of immigration may be a source of strain in that it multiplies problems of enculturation and social control.

An ideal wife was required to conform to a number of detailed and not always consistent criteria. She was supposed to be from the same village as her husband; she was supposed to be a sister's daughter (failing that a mother's brother's daughter or a father's sister's daughter); she was expected to be younger than the groom, from a relatively poor family, fair of skin, hard-working, com-

Table 1.—Authority relationships showing similarity of obligations and behaviors. Authority: all called *"yajaman."*

	Wife	Son	Younger brother	Servant	Low-caste	Villager
Punishment by yajaman:						
Beats	x	x	x	x	x	x
Expels	x	x	x	x	x	x
Denies food	x	x	x	x	x	
Refuses credit . . .				x	x	x
Appropriate protest by subordinate:						
Sulking	x	x	x	x	x	x
Remonstrating . . .	x	x	x	x	x	x
Running away . . .	x	x	x	x	x	x
Suicide	x	x	x	x	x	x
Shirking or withdrawing services .	x	x	x	x	x	x
May damage yajaman by:						
Stealing	x	x	x	x	x	x
Complaining to higher authority	x	x	x	x	x	x
"Poisoning"	x					
Transmitting pollution	x			x	x	
Failing to pay taxes .						x
Serves yajaman by:						
Work and obedience	x	x	x	x	x	x
Aiding in ceremonial	x	x	x	x	x	x
Receives from yajaman:						
Food or grain . . .	x	x	x	x	x	x
Clothing	x	x	x	x	x	
Shelter	x	x	x	x		
Arrangement of marriage . . .		x	x	x		
Regulation of marriage					x	x
Credit				x	x	x
Advice and spiritual training	x	x	x	x	x	x
Conciliation and support in disputes . .	x	x	x	x	x	x

pletely devoted, virgin, docile, beautiful, and thoroughly familiar with all wifely duties. Such a wife could never be more than a young man's dream, but most bridegrooms are young men.

In real life, many of the criteria for the proper wife can be realized only rarely. A wife can come from the same village as her husband only if she belongs to a different lineage and only if she is of an appropriate age and relationship. The smaller the village and the more castes it has, the fewer the opportunities for intravillage marriages. A wife can rarely be both a sister's daughter and a member of a poor family because, assuming that the sister's husband has been chosen in accordance with the rules, the sister's daughter would be of a wealthier family. The probability that any given male will have available to him a suitable sister's daughter, mother's brother's daughter, or father's sister's daughter is difficult to calculate. In Mysore State, where Namhalli is located, the available data indicate that less than one fifth of all marriages are with such close relatives.

Differences in age between bride and groom, ranging from five to eighteen years when extreme cases are disregarded, may also have been a source of strain. In many cases the husband had to postpone his marriage until he was twenty-five or thirty years old, and then postpone consummation of his marriage until the bride was old enough, usually 16 years. Young men were by no means sexually deprived. They obtained satisfaction from prostitutes in many cases, but they also slept with the wives or daughters of their fellow villagers. Exact figures concerning the number of women who had sexual experience before marriage or the number of wives who were unfaithful cannot be given, but it is certain that anxieties about postmarital and premarital fidelity create friction in a great many marital relationships in Namhalli.

While many marriages, even in Namhalli, seem to have survived the discovery that the wife or husband was less than ideal, there were further causes of anxiety within the relationship. One of these was the wife's capacity to damage her husband. She may pollute him and cause him to lose his caste if she sleeps with or takes food from a person of lower caste. She can pollute him with her own menstrual fluid or by putting improper substances in his food. In some cases, wives stand accused of accidentally or deliberately "poisoning" their husbands. The wife attracts her husband away from the things of the spirit, and causes him to waste his semen, considered a vital substance for both material and spiritual advancement. Children, borne by the wife, burden the husband with further material cares.

These many strains within the marital relationship were handled by the mobilization of village and caste authority. The complex marriage ceremony involving bride or groom price, a gift of jewels to the wife, public approval of the match, and careful selection of both bride and groom could also be regarded as a device for helping to stabilize the relationship. Particularly in older times, the prospect of losing the jewelry given at the time of the wedding and having to assemble funds for a second marriage must have encouraged men to maintain good relations with their wives. Unless the wife had a wealthy family that would approve of her conduct, divorce might well leave her without property, without children other than nursing children, and without any other means of support than begging or prostitution. Despite the elaborate machinery designed to promote stable marriages, separation, desertion, and divorce are much more frequent than people in Namhalli think they should be.

People living in Namhalli in 1952 and 1953 had few memories of any major conflicts that had taken place in the village in earlier times. Memory tends to linger upon cooperative undertakings, upon the role of the Headman in settling arguments and controlling improper behavior, and upon the need to maintain village solidarity in the face of a hostile and somewhat mysterious outside world. The relatively small size of the community also supports the idea that there was little overt conflict, for even today such small villages tend to be conservative and to display little interest in public disputes of the kind that lead to official notice of the village. Further, whether or not there was conflict, it is apparent that such conflict as there was did not interfere with public projects such as digging wells, constructing irrigation works, maintaining village fortifications, or holding village-wide ceremonies.

The successful carrying out of community-wide projects and the corresponding absence of reported factionalist dispute can be attributed to the presence of strong authority, to the small size of the village, and to the lack of any clear lines of cleavage along which the community might have been divided. According to the *Sukraniti*, "Discord must never be created between husband and wife, master and servant, brother and brother, preceptor and pupil, ... father and sons." Strains were present and recognized in both the community and the sacred literature, but there were established means of preventing the development of overt conflict around such points of strain.

Perhaps the most interesting aspect of strain in Namhalli is that most of the identifiable strains can be linked together and related to major ideological principles, such as the unreality of the perceptual world and the contrast between principles of hierarchy and equality. These principles lead to the notion of separate moral and practical obligations attached to each social relationship (dharma *vs.* karma) and, therefore, to the necessity of specifying obligations in great detail. The fact that obligations cannot be so specified leads to a need for strong authority to legislate and enforce specific obligations in specific situations. It is also worth noting that all authority relationships are based upon approximately the same principles and are referred to by the same term, *yajaman*. This means that the weakening of any single hierarchic relationship is a weakening of all hierarchic relationships. Like most authoritarian organizations, traditional Namhalli had two unsolved problems: the timely and efficient replacement of ineffective leaders, and coping with situations in which the leaders had no power to enforce their authority.

3. *The Background of Conflict in Taos*

Taos, like Namhalli, is a village, and like Namhalli it must conform to the culture of the surrounding region. However, unlike Namhalli, the pueblo retains important elements of a tribal orientation. Cities were not a part of its cultural heritage as either administrative or market centers. They came to play a role in its more recent history, but only as excrescences—as something and somebodies out there—and not as centers that integrated and codified its tradition. Unlike Namhalli, therefore, Taos produced goods almost exclusively for local use and not for an urban center.

Archeological and ethnological evidence tells us that Taos's ancestors were probably from two branches of a stream of settlers having a common cultural background, who settled in the basin of the Rio Grande and its tributaries a few centuries before the arrival of the Spanish in the sixteenth century. Like many similar neighboring communities, Taos and its pueblo relatives maintained staunch feelings of physical and cultural independence. Although each pueblo had to act to some extent in recognition of the presence and character of the others, it conducted itself on the whole independently, as if the behavior and ideology of its members were all its own, and as if it had been forced to solve its own problems in a state of complete isolation. There is only occasional visiting between pueblos, even today, and this pattern appears to be of long duration. Indeed, visits must have been even more infrequent when transportation was by foot or horse.

Both the earlier and the present-day villages of Taos were located on a tributary of the Rio Grande that flows through a small plain along the eastern foothills of the Sangre de Cristo range. The

historic pueblo is nestled at the base of a heavily wooded mountain, at an elevation of over 7,000 feet above sea level, and is bi-
sected by a stream that provides a permanent water supply. The
soil is predominantly sedimentary, brought down and deposited
by the mountain stream, and comprises gravels, sands, and clays
covering the valley floor. It is a rich soil for cultivation, and it also
provides excellent material for adobe blocks and bricks, which are
used with wood for construction. Although the high altitude limits
the growing period to about ninety days, the pueblo was able to
grow all the food it needed until the time when the population
began a steady increase and the amount of arable land diminished.
Small game, especially deer and rabbits, has always been abundant.

Moisture conditions present certain problems in the area, since
the length of the rainy season is variable, but there have been no
periods of extended drought or famine. In fact, prior to the curtailment of land in post-Spanish times, a combination of rich soil, adequate moisture under controlled conditions, and a flexible zone of
exploitation enabled the village to attain a sizable population, perhaps two or three thousand persons when first discovered.

Long, cold winters with heavy snowfalls must have impeded
transportation and communication between Taos and other settlements, especially during the days of foot travel. Even today there
are periods when the modern road between Taos and Picuris, the
nearest pueblo neighbor, is virtually impassable. Otherwise, the
open plains to the east, and various valleys and passes, tended to
facilitate transportation, and indeed regular contact was established with Apaches and other nonpueblo peoples. But the polity
of each settlement was independent of the others; there were in
earlier times, as now, no established mechanisms for developing or
maintaining intergroup cooperative functions such as mutual defense, economic exchange, or communication. Marriages were con-
tracted between Taos citizens, and also with the Apache and with
some of the neighboring pueblos, but we have no way of knowing
with what frequency.

As long as memory extends, Taos has been largely endogamous.

Marriages that brought in alien men have been particularly frowned upon because of the newcomers' ignorance of theological and ritual traditions. Little more than a decade ago, in fact, the village council took action to oust all such men from the pueblo. This action occurred during a crisis in the authority relationship between the old men and the "boys," and similar action appears to have been taken under stress in the past. Given the general suspicion that has prevailed toward nonmembers, it is likely that exogamy has never occurred on a large scale, and that endogamy has long been preferred as it is now.

Apart from the few exogamous marriages, the only regular intercourse between Taos and other pueblos was connected with ceremonial-festival occasions. From these, a certain number of personal alliances developed between pueblos, but on only one occasion did they lead to an intervillage political alliance, during the Pueblo Revolt of 1680. The "friend" relationship has a long history at Taos, and in recent times it has been extended and intensified as a result of contacts established in the Indian boarding schools. An inter-pueblo organization known as the All-Pueblo Council was established about a generation ago. It meets regularly and brings together a select number of persons who are the most politically active in Indian affairs from all the pueblos. The relationships established do not have the intimate quality of school ties, which are formed at an earlier and more impressionable age, and only a small fraction of school friends are brought together in this way. The council has not succeeded in establishing itself as a federation. Like the United Nations, it is an institution in which issues of common interest can be discussed by completely autonomous member states.

The first settlers in Taos several centuries ago brought with them a fairly elaborate set of beliefs and an organizational system related to the role of supernatural powers in human affairs. Judging from archeological evidence, most of the ritual apparatus, if not the entire belief system, had been worked out some time before the present pueblo was settled. In the more recent past it has functioned largely in relation to weather control and propitiation, and the control of fowl and wild game. Elsewhere among the eastern pueblos it is closely linked to customs and beliefs of disease and curing, and this may well have been the case at Taos also in earlier times.

TECHNOLOGICAL SOLUTIONS

When the first settlers came to Taos they raised the usual crops of that region—maize, beans, cotton, gourds, and tobacco—and probably then as now hunted rabbits, deer, and antelope. To these were added in post-Spanish times certain grains, animals, and fruit of European or Mexican origin—wheat, melons, apples, peaches, tomatoes, and chili, as well as goats, sheep, and chickens. The traditional crops required nothing more than a simple digging stick for planting, a one-person task. To augment the water supply from the uncertain rainfall, small-scale hydraulic works were developed. This meant ditching, clearing, terracing, damming, and braking, all of which required considerable cooperative effort, distribution of functions, scheduling, and regulation of the water supply. With new crops and domesticated animals the Spanish also introduced such new techniques and tools as hoes, plows, saddles, bridles, harnesses, axes, shovels, and metal knives.

As at Namhalli, certain methods of coping directly with food-producing requirements were characteristic of the region, but they did not necessitate a set of interdependent relations among communities. Here again, each pueblo was self-sufficient. For a time after livestock grazing had been introduced by the Spanish, however, a certain amount of cooperation among pueblos occurred, and equipment and certain other objects of utility (e.g., metal knives or shovels) had to be obtained outside the village. Eventually, each pueblo built up its own herds and began to trade independently. Traditional agriculture could be practiced with little if any specialization, except along age-sex lines, and Indian men are still, on the whole, jacks-of-all-trades and seldom specialists in any. The Cacique, perhaps, is partly supported by community surplus, and there are a few families that make a livelihood as traders and storekeepers. At wheat-planting time and harvesting time, when the hoeing of large maize plots has to be done, the family recruits additional hands from among adults of both sexes within the kindred. At neighboring Picuris Pueblo, the few remaining active farmers are ashamed of being forced to hire Spanish neighbors for this purpose.

In proto-historic and historic times, coping with enemies posed greater problems. Raiding Apaches and probably other Plains Indians were destructive, or at least worrisome. We know little specifically about the pre-Spanish mobilization and effectiveness of fighting manpower in the face of such raids or in open warfare. It can be surmised, however, from the survival of the offices of war chiefs (who exercise no military functions today) that defense was handled in some direct way. It is probable that both the height of the buildings and the thickness of the adobe walls helped the pueblo to withstand many direct attacks. Several centuries ago the pueblo was relocated from a rather open area to a protected cul-de-sac up against the mountain wall. Partly the move seems to have been made to gain additional water supply from mountain streams, but the new location may also have provided greater defensive advantage against surprise attack. Plains Indians were certainly closer to Taos and Picuris than to other pueblos, and methods of fighting were undoubtedly diffused from the former to the latter (as witness the memory at Taos and the actual remains at Picuris of a scalp house). However, the distance separating Plains and Pueblo people was still great enough to preclude frequent skirmishes. At any rate the village prospered, met this periodic threat effectively, and at the time of the first Spanish visitors was in a state of vigor and vitality. Because of the requirements of agriculture as developed in pueblo communities, intervillage contact appears to have involved very little open conflict. Nor did it lead to defensive or aggressive coalitions until the uprising against Spanish domination in 1680.

These technological solutions to primary problems posed by external conditions created second-order problems concerned with the organization requirements of irrigation and water rights. Irrigation, as we have seen, necessitated some means of ensuring communal effort. Traditionally, little food surplus was accumulated, and limited cooperation would suffice as long as hydraulic procedures were effectively coordinated. Crops of European origin, such as wheat, are produced in surplus, however, and in order to obtain a greater return on this surplus, the same social technique used in irrigation could be extended to the use of communal granaries, which make possible the storing of grain until it commands peak price in the market. Earlier it could also be extended to mobilize defense efforts.

IDEOLOGICAL SOLUTIONS

The system of beliefs that supports and complements the technological system is relatively consistent and simple compared with that of Namhalli. The strains inherent in it result from the fact that it only partly solved problems of explanation. From the time the Taos dwellers first settled in their present location, technological and empirically verified knowledge enabled them to solve their problems successfully at a given level and under stable and generally predictable external conditions, but the knowledge was inadequate in extraordinary times. The water supply was adequate for the crops they raised, but only if it was properly husbanded and carefully used. If the volume of water in a given year was little more than the minimum required, regulatory mechanisms might not always succeed. Even when men have done the proper things, planted with the best skills available, including since the eighteenth century the use of iron plows, hoes, shovels, and certain machinery, they are still dependent upon natural elements other than water. The growing season is short, and in some years there might not be enough sun, or heavy downpours might come at the wrong times. Furthermore, the land available to a family might be adequate in one generation, but inadequate for the next, when numbers have increased. Whereas land resources prior to Western contact could be expanded as needed, for nearly the past three hundred years they have been restricted in one way or another.

The set of beliefs that related the heavens to the earth, to the underworld, and to man was intended originally to explain success and failure in a society that depended exclusively on horticulture

and a little hunting for its food. This body of understanding has
been maintained and even reinforced in the face of external pressures as a means of symbolizing cultural identity. Owing to its long
history it has not developed any apparent intrinsic inconsistencies.

It is believed that if people follow the rules of those who have
come to know, if they submit to training and acquire knowledge
themselves, if they cooperate with others in the performance of
rituals designed to channel supernatural powers to support human
effort, and if they refrain from competitive actions in performing
everyday tasks and extend cooperative effort to all technical problems, then natural forces will tend to work in favor of man. We
shall probably never know with certainty more than a small part
of the complex set of beliefs and understandings that make up the
Taos conception of the supernatural and its relation to men and
to things. It seems clear however, that it tends to deal with the relation of spiritual powers and beings to specific categories of direct
experience, such as rain and snow, sickness and death, the growing
of maize, the qualities of animals, and the requirements for a successful hunt. Priestly functionaries have never been free to develop
a theology that systematically related isolated fragments and patterns of belief, and established a coherent view of the universe.
The religion is little concerned with ultimate meanings or subtle
transcendental explanations of the nature of life.

Thus for the Taos citizen there is no conflict of belief such as
the Indian villager must contend with in reconciling the real and
phenomenal worlds. Only one set of standards governs the relations of man to nature, of man to man, and of man and nature to
spiritual powers. In turn, spiritual powers help or hinder persons,
or the group collectively, in accordance with performance measured by these standards. Explanations relating behavior in these
several domains are thus circular and interdependent. All men, as
they mature, acquire increasing mastery over a common body of
understanding about cosmological forces and the spirit powers of
the sun, moon, and so on, beliefs that complement their technological mastery and account for their success or failure in coping
with environmental circumstances.

Taos culture can in this sense be said to be highly integrated, but inconsistencies have arisen between the traditional belief system and the technological order with which it is historically associated. New elements have been added to the system in the wake of new external realities. Restricted land resources have involved an ever-increasing number of persons in a technological system whose requirements differ from those of traditional pueblo culture. Hence there is a real ideological strain between the older elements of belief and the more recent elements, since they have had to find solutions to different coexisting sets of problems. Security traditionally grows from identification with one's own kind—in this case, other Taos Indians—as certain things gradually come to be accepted as true beliefs about the good person. At the very least, then, even assuming that some amount of ambivalence exists, members of the tribe must conform to understandings about the legitimate exercise of authority, and must respond to demands for participation in ceremonial life.

Taos shares with other pueblos of the region a very old set of beliefs that to some extent cope indirectly with environmental problems where direct methods prove to be imperfect. It explains what is necessary for successful productive effort and gives reasons why some effort is unsuccessful. Despite the greatest care and skill, a maize crop, for example, might suffer from frost in late summer or early autumn, deer might elude the hunter or accidents befall him. The village might be carefully planned and its dwellings well-built for defense in case of attack, but the inhabitants might still occasionally be caught scattered in the fields or off guard, and suffer severe losses. Against illnesses, certain pharmaceutica and other healing techniques about which we know very little similarly provided people with a limited guarantee against sudden, unexpected death.

Second, beginning with the post-contact period, Taos acquired additional solutions to old problems—namely, new crops for agricultural enterprise and additional sources of energy (animal, then machine power)—and subsequently new problems and social techniques (for example, teaching new skills and providing new occupational alternatives). These led to the development of beliefs about the efficacy and desirability of the technological innovations and their associated behavioral adaptations. Animal husbandry requires decisions about alternative uses of a limited zone of cultivation, including whether to grow a certain proportion of Old World grains instead of maize. Climatic requirements for growing and harvesting of these crops involve partly different explanations for success or failure of the operations. Reliance upon wage labor and the demand for one's skills involves risk, but it also allows greater freedom of movement and variety of experience, and supplements reduced returns from the land. The things one can do or acquire oneself become linked to beliefs about the rights of individuals, and also to concepts of respective spheres of authority and control.

Finally, since the older and newer elements of belief and understanding are often inconsistent, the villagers are confronted with ideological strain. Perhaps it would be more correct to say that the elders and the farmer-priests are intransigent in the face of nontraditional behavior, which goes against central or core beliefs. It follows that when men act in an untraditional way, they are made to feel that they are disobeying the wishes of the hierarchy. They are expected to know what the true ideology is and what it requires, or at least, if they do not know, to accept whatever is told them by persons who are more versed in sacred knowledge until they acquire wisdom. Anything that might distract attention from the distinctive symbols of Taos culture is likely to be construed as non-Indian, hence undesirable and proscribed. There is no denying that new problems have arisen, forcing accommodations of belief and commitment, but changes come slowly at Taos, and no new elements are recognized until control and interpretation have been reasserted.

Rewards are considered the result of acquired virtuous behavior, adequate training by parents and other teachers, and proper socialization of the young. Crop failure, illness, and other unforeseen events are believed to be the result of individual failure to act virtuously, or of failure by the group as a whole to perform symbolic (ceremonial) acts meant to ensure the continued functioning of spirit and celestial powers on behalf of man.

There is a fine balance between retribution, suffered either by the individual or the entire community, and inappropriate behavior. Retribution can mean crop failures and thus threaten the very survival of the community. Citizens are expected to act in accordance with the same rules of conduct that prevailed when they were predominantly self-subsistent agriculturalists, lest such misfortunes as faulty distribution and regulation of the water supply or loss of land befall one and all.

SOCIAL SOLUTIONS

Today in Taos, technological and ideological methods of coping with environmental conditions demand a close and constant scrutiny of behavior, and another set of standards must exist for behavior outside the pueblo. One's conduct with "friends," acquaintances, and employers outside the pueblo is proper to those relationships only, and has no connection with how one acts within the pueblo. Though a man may work outside the pueblo, he is expected to arrange his work so as to leave time for community obligations, and if he is not readily available when summoned or if he is suspected of having weakened the power of the group by becoming too friendly with outsiders, he will be criticized for his conduct. Both the family and ceremonial societies may be hampered in the performance of their tasks by this sort of behavior, and therefore certain controls have been established to ensure effective participation in them.

In Taos persons charged with the authority to exercise this control, which implies punishing offenders, are, at the top, the heads of kiva societies, with secular officers under them, chosen from the ranks of middle-aged and older male household heads. These men have the experience, learning, and wisdom to judge the virtue of the actions of others, and to make the many, often delicate, decisions on which the fate of the community depends. They instruct during kiva training; they place the guilt for and resolve quarrels in the public interest; and they make final decisions about matters not covered by precedent. For example, today they must decide whether or not electricity can be installed, a road paved, or a non-Indian social dance held.

The social structure of Taos is rather simple, compared with Namhalli's. Community organization reflects both strong centripetal and centrifugal forces, in which the differences of interest between individuals and groups are overcome through a series of ever-widening spheres of power and authority. The assumption and exercise of decision-making tends to be based upon the following principles: older over younger, male over female, higher-ranking families (in the ceremonies) over lower, and ritually trained or more knowledgeable over ritually untrained or less knowledgeable.

The composition and ideal operation of the Pueblo Council will reflect both how these principles are supposed to operate and some major sources of strain in the system. Early in the seventeenth century the Spanish imposed a system of civil government on the pueblos, primarily to establish a mechanism for communication and allocating responsibility in their relations with the Indians. Although there is now a formal distinction between "sacred" and "secular" offices, which is reflected in the composition of the council, traditional principles govern the way in which the council operates.

A full council consists of the following four classes of members: (1) the governor and lieutenant governor, annually elected (sometimes including by invitation the members of his staff); (2) the war captain and lieutenant war captain (and occasionally, also by invitation, the members of his staff); (3) *principales*, who are all individuals formerly elected to the above offices; and (4) the Cacique, a hereditary office, and chiefs of the six currently functioning kiva societies. The total number of active council members may vary from about 30 to 40, depending upon how many assistants to the governor and the war captain are invited to participate.

There is a more fundamental dual composition, with the members of class 4 as one group and the remaining members as another. Parsons (1939) writes that, prior to the establishment of present secular offices by the Spanish, the Taos council consisted only of the chiefs of the kiva societies. Today they serve as staff to the Cacique, and in effect choose or control their successors. Together with the Cacique they are the effective government. Any of these men can be nominated for governor, in which case sacred and secular power coincide in the same person. The validation of power then approximates that of an earlier day, in which authority was delegated to men who had achieved much learning in the sacred belief system and experience in directing ceremonials, and who were as a rule, therefore, elders.

The Taos river bisects the central portion of the village, which lies inside an encircling adobe wall. The six functioning kiva societies are situated three on either side of the stream; but for ceremonial and political purposes three kiva groups, two on one side and one on the other, are aligned as "male" and three as "female." The final nominations for governor (two candidates are chosen at this time) take place at meetings that are convened in what appear to be the ranking kivas of the two groups. In recent years the three female kivas have met in Big Earring kiva to decide upon their candidate, and the three male kivas meet similarly in Water People kiva with its headman as host. The Cacique himself may nominate a third candidate. A convention is then held in Big Earring kiva with the headman of that society as host and the Cacique presiding. It is here that final eliminations take place and the governor for the following year is chosen. On such occasions, as well as at regular council meetings, the Cacique, acting as presiding official, is charged with seeing that arguments and decisions proceed in an orderly fashion. In the end there must be unanimity, which ideally is achieved by the giving in of the minority who are in disagreement. When strong differences are known to exist, either a few dissenters avoid possibly embarrassing situations by failing to attend a given meeting, or a controlling person or kiva society will simply not notify certain councilors who are known to have taken strong opposing positions. In theory, of course, all groups and chiefs should have an equal voice in proceedings. Each should be considerate of the feelings and opinions of others. Personal differences, strengths, weaknesses, abilities, or inadequacies, however, produce in fact a variety of possible outcomes. Shortly after World War II, for example, a strong-willed kiva chief was able to dominate much of the proceedings of the council because of

the weakness of the Cacique. The office of Cacique is hereditary
in the male line, and an incumbent holds the office until he is
deemed incapable of discharging his duties (capability being defined generously). If the Cacique is weak and the kiva chief strong,
the kiva chief may go on controlling decisions for too long a time,
postponing the choosing of a new Cacique and successfully staving
off opposition either by the people or by other councilors. Strong-
willed opposition is just as contrary to Taos principles of reasonable
accommodation and considerateness as is strong-willed leadership
on the part of a chief. But if the chief finally loses the respect of the
community by actions that no longer reflect general concerns, his
influence over others will correspondingly diminish, and the situation will tend to be redressed.

In the political structure of the pueblo, therefore, a major source
of strain lies in the discrepancy between norms governing decision-
making procedures and the personal characteristics of incumbents
at any given time. Death may remove from leadership positions
persons who are actually (as they should be) old and wise, and put
into them others who in the normal course of events would have
risen more slowly. Real power lies with the priests, and the government is in fact a theocracy. The priests appoint the governor,
the governor's staff, and all other secular officers (positions that
came into effect with the Spanish Royal Edict of 1621). For more
than three centuries these officers have represented the council in
its relations with the outside world. Presently such relationships
include dealings with the Pueblo Agency or with the federal government in Washington, managing tourist trade, and similar activities. But the priests may also feel impelled to accept nominations
for governor and lieutenant governor. When this happens the
secular government is relatively powerful, and there is little need
to invite the appointed helpers of the appointed officials to attend
council meetings, for they have relatively few duties. "As long as
the headmen remain disinterested, more and more authority dif-
fuses to the governor and his staff" (Fenton, 1957, p. 315).

In other words, minor positions as aides to the major officials are
allotted to the young men. There is no place for them in the theo-

retical power structure, but they are needed in the actual exercise of authority. Strain is implicit in this situation, for young men working their way up as apprentices may feel slighted if they are not asked to attend council meetings. When differences of interest lead to jockeying for power, the governor, in particular, may invite secretaries and other helpers to meetings, and at the same time fail to invite some bona fide councilor. At other times, when the business of the council is running more smoothly (according to ideal norms and dominant values), minor officials will tend to be neglected.

Political roles have assumed an increasing degree of indeterminacy during the period of stress upon which we have concentrated, because several of the council members have little or no command of English. The governor's secretary and interpreter (among the aides) are therefore in a position of potential influence in Taos matters. If the governor desires to assume authority and exercise power, he may use the interpreter to represent his position, as the position of the council, to Agency officials. On other occasions the interpreter can use his office to set forth Agency policy in special ways and so direct pueblo decision along certain lines. Behavioral rules that govern these relationships and the strains they involve are unchanged from those described in the earliest Spanish chronicles.

The strain in the political structure can be viewed, also, in terms of two sets of opposing tendencies: (1) on the one hand the need to solve internal problems of the pueblo, and on the other the need to handle external relations; and (2) on the one hand a strong authority system, and on the other a high respect for cooperation in performing tasks.

Ideally and traditionally the council claims for itself all policy decisions concerning the pueblo as a whole, and delegates only routine matters to the governor and his staff. The governor, similarly, takes action on matters that come to his attention only after referring them to the councilors for policy consideration and recommendations. When he goes to Albuquerque on business transactions with the Pueblo Agency, he is generally accompanied by one or more members of the council. In the pueblo itself the governor has the irksome task of carrying out a great many policy decisions of the council, of exercising seemingly arbitrary authority, and of receiving the brunt of public criticism. He organizes the task forces for sweeping the plaza preparatory to ceremonial performances, repairing and plastering churches, clearing irrigation ditches, and so on. The governor or one of his staff climbs up on a housetop and calls out what work is to be done, by whom, and when. He is also responsible for checking up on delinquents, and for assessing fines on malingerers. For all of this he serves without recompense.

Control over his actions on internal matters can readily be exerted by the councilors if they are so minded. They are less able to exert control on matters outside the wall; and should the governor command sufficient respect to exercise control over decisions in which he sharply differs from others, he may take measures first in this domain. In an earlier day external relations were confined to protection from outside aggression and from trespassers, relatively simple matters to understand and handle. Beginning with the middle of the nineteenth century, these tasks became much more subtle, and therefore more difficult to communicate and administer. From this point of view, the roles of the various members of the hierarchy, though clear in theory, are in practice subject to considerable variation.

Finally, an important source of strain, not only in the political structure but to some extent at all levels, beginning with the household, is the simultaneous respect for authority in hierarchical relationships and for considerateness, cooperation, and unanimity in all human relations. Under favorable circumstances all issues brought before the council are subjected to fair and impartial discussion by all members. The Cacique, we are told, presides at these meetings, where he acts as moderator and sees to it that debate is orderly and well-modulated. After sorting out the arguments he makes a decision and submits it to those assembled. If there is not full agreement, debate is reopened until an interpretation becomes increasingly agreeable to all. The final decision is then conveyed to the governor and his staff.

All have an equal voice in reaching a decision, and even the Cacique as moderator represents the will of the community. If he feels that the public will is about to be violated, he can redirect the question. However, occasionally somebody must resolve differences and force a decision. In this process two factors can contravene desirable procedure: the personalities of the officeholders and the order of opening debate. If the Cacique is weak, he may leave executive matters to one of the stronger headmen, especially if the latter happens to be governor. Emphasis upon conformity only thinly masks underlying aggression (see Parsons, 1936), and the traditional reliance upon authority can lead one or another of the society chiefs to assert his will when power is indeterminate. Furthermore, under such circumstances a host chief has a certain advantage in argument inasmuch as he begins discussion. A forceful argument by a man who is inclined to assert leadership (for whatever personal reasons) can often align others who act more out of deference to considerateness and cooperation.

Whereas the balance between the principles of hierarchy and cooperation can in a sense be thought of as mutually redressing the conflicts engendered by either acted upon independently, we can observe how commitment to both ideals is in itself a potential source of conflict. Acknowledgment of a strong, clearly understood hierarchy of authoritative figures has been an important means of dealing with threats to the existence of the group, whether imaginary or real, as long as this problem was perceived as unyielding and ever-present. In Taos, however, as at Namhalli, the problem of defense was solved in part by the nucleated village, which undoubtedly caused people to feel that agreement and accommodation, if not friendship, were necessary to cope with the secondary problem of intensive interaction and close physical proximity. Agreement and cooperation traditionally were reinforced without a resort to sanctions by a strong preference for local endogamy. It is somewhat ironic and characteristic of the central paradox at Taos that cooperation should periodically be dictated by fiat—for example, by the demand that all spouses of nonpueblo origin leave the community.

Training in both authoritarianism and submergence of the individual will to group interests begins in the household, which consists ideally of the nuclear family, but is often augmented by widowed parents or aunts, orphaned cousins, and, occasionally, adopted children. Residence is usually neolocal, although often out of choice or necessity the home of a newly married couple will be built adjacent to the home of one of the couple's parents. In any event lineal and collateral relatives live close to one another throughout their lifetimes.

Each groom upon marriage becomes head of his own household, and wields strong authoritarian control over the behavior of all members. On the other hand, productive property—land or other forms of family capital, like livestock—is owned by wives as well as by husbands, and all children are supposed to inherit equally. The father has rights of disposal, but responsibilities to his children and the scarcity of land in effect make him a custodian rather than a controller of property. In the face of actual needs—that is, the need to enable one or a few children to acquire minimum holdings to continue farming—the principle of shared rights and of recourse to paternal rights of disposal can lead to family conflicts. The nuclear family and shared inheritance were only compatible with agricultural productivity when the population remained stable or grew slowly, and when the amount of arable land could be varied to suit village needs. The need to bequeath differentially might lead to dissension among the members of the family about working as a unit in the common enterprise of farming. Questions of inheritance, indeed, have long been the chief cause of family quarrels (Parsons, 1936, p. 52).

The quality of the husband-wife relationship itself must be viewed in relation to hierarchical and collateral principles of association. In general, marriages tend to be stable, and divorce is rare and disapproved. The governor may bring pressure on a couple whose marital problems have come to public attention. Close kinsmen of both parties may also exert more informal pressures for reconciliation. On the other hand, it is usual and expected for husbands to treat their wives without consideration in such matters as disposition of personal property, the treatment of children, or the performance of tasks in the family. Quarrels of this sort are deplored, but deference is generally given to the dominance of husbands over wives, unless the latter are physically abused. The low rate of separation or divorce is probably also related to the large number of kindred that spouses share in a highly endogamous community.

The subordination of females to males is reflected in all areas of public life. Girls and women remain closely attached to the home from childhood, tending the gardens close to the house and only occasionally leaving home to visit and help prepare for feasts. With the growth of the Anglo town of Taos an increasing number of women have found work as domestic servants or as waitresses. Even so this amounts to no more than five per cent of the adult female population. Women make most of the daily domestic decisions, but on the whole their behavior is constrained, and they are permitted little exercise of imagination. Nevertheless, their training for adult roles is consistent, continuously goal-directed, and secure within its realm.

If the range of viable alternatives is expanded by changing experience outside the pueblo, strains may develop in male-female roles and interaction. Female models for all but a few have a very narrow base, and the roles of girls and women are very much alike: acquiring and performing domestic skills, caring for the young, organizing and executing home-centered ceremonials, and, for some, spending a variable amount of time on highly specific tasks outside the village. Within the pueblo itself females are excluded from all important phases of participation in ceremonial life and from any power positions that involve knowledge appropriate to the direction of ritual activities. They are given minimum training in the character and importance of basic beliefs. They are taught certain ceremonial dances and are required to take part in them. Their very ignorance, limited participation in sacred activities, and instruction on the importance of secrecy and occult values combine to make the women uniformly even more conservative and emotionally committed than the men. Their domain is a separate-valued category of activities in which they alone are proficient.

Life may be less varied and exciting than it is for males, but it has its own rewards. What is more important, there are no other goals to which they look forward at any age. Unlike the "boys," the un-initiated or inexperienced, they cannot anticipate entry into more important and powerful public positions. To alter substantially this state of affairs, specifically to make aspirations for females a matter of choice, would be to revolutionize the social system and the value system upon which it rests. For this kind of innovation there are as yet no vocal advocates.

Strain in the father-son relation is inherent in its nurturant and authoritative components, which also change in practice with the age of the father. Young fathers possess traditional authority, and this increases with age and especially with ritual experience and community service. They are at the same time, however, subordi-nate to the political power of older men. Fathers are expected to take the part of their sons in arguing certain claims before the coun-cil, and they also constitute the first line of appeal by young men in cases of conflict with social norms. But as they mature and be-come more responsibly involved in community affairs, they must face certain difficult conflicts of interests and loyalties. The agonies created by the introduction of peyote activities dramatize the sig-nificance of these hierarchic-collateral principles in the mainte-nance of community structure.

Normally the conflicts caused by social strains could be regu-lated by jural authorities, whose hands were strengthened by such ever-present threats to the village as bad weather, the imperfect predictability of seasonal changes, and the arbitrary decisions (from the pueblo viewpoint) of outside authorities. Disobedience might bring dire consequences not only upon the individual or his family, but also upon the entire community. In an earlier day whipping was a common punishment for failure to comply with summons to work on public enterprises (such as repairing of ir-rigation ditches) or to participate in ceremonials. Nowadays fines are substituted for public whippings. The governor has the author-ity to levy fines and jail individuals who are guilty of misconduct, drunkenness, or disorderly behavior, and he is prepared to exercise it with a heavy hand. The readiness to accede to this authority is a measure of the anxiety that confronts most persons when they contemplate facing alone these dangers of the world about them. A young woman now in her twenties relates how she suffered from hysterical paralysis of the right arm and hand when her parents took her outside the pueblo at the age of six for an indefinite sojourn in the outside world. Such fear, generally present in the village, can be utilized when conflict threatens to increase and decisions are questioned. On those occasions the elders have been able to assert their authority effectively by resurrecting the specter of taxation and ultimate loss of land. Loss of self-control by the individual (especially aggressive, incautious behavior) and challenging the jural rights of legitimate authorities—in short, a failure to present a united front as continuously as possible against external dangers—would severely undermine the effectiveness of the "men." They alone can deal with government officials beyond the wall of the village. They alone are capable of preserving and transmitting the ideological knowledge that supports the technological basis of traditional society.

4. Strain

The foregoing descriptions of Namhalli and Taos should indicate that all cultural systems have established characteristics that predispose them toward particular kinds and degrees of conflict. In discussing the various ways and means of directly and indirectly coping with problems posed by external conditions, we have depicted both communities as firmly established and highly organized systems. In a sense, this model of a "relatively steady state" is absolutely necessary as a starting point for any discussion of change or movement. The concept of strain, to be defined shortly, is based upon the assumption that the very process of establishing organized and stable relationships with the surroundings perpetuates or develops areas of life that are comparatively *less* organized and *less* stable. In a truly steady state, there could be no foreshadowing of future changes, since there would be a one-to-one correspondence of the parts. The concept of strain provides a means of having one's steady state and changing it too, for strain implies a hierarchy of steadiness within the steady state such that, granted changes in relationships to external conditions, some things are more likely to change than others.

Briefly, strain has to do with those areas of life in which culturally induced expectations tend to be frustrated most frequently. In terms of the historical development of a particular organization, interaction between the organizational membership and the environment leads to the development of a cultural tradition that includes various formulae designed to solve recurrent problems. Such formulae appear to be of two general kinds: direct or pragmatic, and indirect or projective. Direct solutions lead to an increase in predictability, so that expectations are met rather frequently, whereas indirect solutions do not lead to an increase in predictability but, rather, conceal unpredictability and cushion the impact of the inevitable defeat of the expectations of those who attempt such solutions.

The emphasis here upon choice behavior and upon predictability leads to a correspondence between the concept of strain and the dissonance theory developed by Leon Festinger (1957, 1964). Our model derives from a concept of choice and predictability in social and cultural systems rather than from the cognitive processes involved in individual behavior. From a developmental standpoint, cultural traditions are formed partly by successful direct attacks upon problems presented by the external world (stresses) and partly by the resolution of dissonances caused by unsuccessful attempts at direct solution. Somewhat pessimistically, then, we assume the universality of failure. If there were a cultural tradition containing answers to every known problem, it could be expected that its membership would soon find additional problems, some of which would turn out to be insoluble. Such problems, because they would give rise to expectations that could not be met, would constitute strains.

Although changing external conditions may cause formerly effective solutions to become less important or less effective, true predictability will generally be a result of true understanding. Therefore, changing external conditions will probably bear with most force upon those areas where problems are indirectly solved and where culturally induced expectations are most rarely met. Where direct solutions become difficult because of difficult external conditions or lack of access to an appropriate stockpile of such solutions, it can be anticipated that people will develop a range of indirect and largely projective solutions as suggested by Wallace (1961, p. 147). Such solutions, to the extent that they fail to render external conditions predictable, will lead to additional situations in which the experience and expectations of one person are in some way counter to those of the organization or of other persons within it. Given a general human tendency to expect that things are predictable even when they are not—a strain toward predictability, to paraphrase Sumner—it may be predicted that the real-life failure of culturally induced expectations will create further problems on the social or the ideological level. Where the problem encountered is truly insolvable, the adoption of individualistic solutions by the membership creates fresh problems of social control and organization. One solution, at a sociological level, is to allow conflict to develop but to introduce legal and ideological devices for resolving it. Another and apparently equally effective method is to create a fictitious reality in which real-life failures are obscured by ideological interpretations.

Strain consists of those recurrent situations in which culturally endorsed predictions fail. Strain may be defined in several additional ways: as a potential conflict within the organization; as a general inability to predict the outcome of certain types of situations; and as situations in which a person sees his expectations defeated. To this list might be added French's definition of ambiguity as a "lack of clarity with regard to appropriate behavior" (1962, p. 238). We feel that these definitions reflect different ways of looking at the same thing. In any case there is little point in multiplying such distinctions unless they can be shown to have theoretical relevance and utility in prediction.

Because unpredicted events occur universally, all human cultures must contain strains. Important differences exist in the amount of strain present in different cultures and in the distribution of particular strains. In theory, the incidence of strain can be measured by the frequency with which individuals find their expectations defeated in various types of situations. So far, attempts at such systematic measurement are notably absent. More common, and unquestionably useful, is the impressionistic enumeration of the major strains apparent within any particular culture. We have given this type of description of Namhalli and Taos in the preceding chapters. For the most part, we have been able to do little more than indicate some of the places where strains appear to occur in considerable number and strength. Namhalli and Taos hardly include all the kinds of strain that can occur or all the ways in which strains can be interrelated to form systematic patterns. A summary and discussion of the major kinds of strain noted in these two communities may nevertheless illustrate some possible classes of strain.

TECHNOLOGICAL STRAINS

Strains that seem to occur in relationships between organizations and their external conditions are defined as technological strains. Both Namhalli and Taos appear to have been successful in establishing stable and systematic relationships with the world around them. In many ways the patterns of relationship established by the two communities are similar. Both use an agricultural technology to produce their basic food requirements. Both appear to have achieved a control over ecological factors adequate to prevent any serious threat to the survival of the community by failures of production. Food production and production in general are one problem that both communities have solved pragmatically. At the same time neither has achieved a perfect solution. There are good and bad years, and good and bad luck, in both places. Neither provides equal rewards to individual members, in the sense that neither succeeds in predicting the amount of harvest a person will obtain from a given amount of labor. In both communities these failures of prediction are explained away by elaborate rituals and ideologies.

Namhalli appears to face two problems that are absent at Taos. Since Taos traditionally lacked outside support, it was unable to permit itself the luxury of crop failure. Such failure was a part of traditional circumstances at Namhalli, and was dealt with by patterns of migration and trade. Where Taos produced most of its own needs, Namhalli relied upon trade for part of its food and other items. Whether Namhalli had crop failures because it could rely upon support from neighboring communities and a regional political organization, or whether it developed relationships with other communities in order to deal with problems like famine, is a moot question. However, eliminating the need for extensive storage of food permits maintenance of a larger population, since the amount of food lost in storage is reduced.

Both communities had to adjust to the seasonal requirements of grain crops, although the adjustments made by the two communities differed markedly. Namhalli's complex system of hierarchic and specialized statuses apparently provided, among its other functions, for seasonal variations in labor needs. Taos appears to have approached the same problem by providing a wide range of alternative roles that each person was supposed to be able to fulfill. There were few full-time specialists at Taos, and most persons filled their year by moving from one occupation to another. In both cases the adjustment of roles and statuses to agricultural problems made it difficult to maintain other types of relationships. Neither community could take full advantage of special abilities or talents that might be developed by its individual members. Although their solutions to the problem of labor needs can be regarded as direct or pragmatic, it is clear that these solutions created a number of additional problems. The organization of irrigation practices at Taos made appropriate conformity to the regulation of water rights uncertain. The result was a degree of unpredictability about the effectiveness with which certain tasks would be performed, or even whether they would be performed at all.

Taos and Namhalli appear to have solved the problem of protection from armed attack in much the same way, by developing nucleated and more or less fortified communities. In neither community could the person working on a distant field be assured of protection, or complete confidence be placed in the defensive measures. In both communities a quasimilitary posture was adopted, based on the strong centralization of authority and the institutionalization of aggressive attitudes toward outsiders and cooperative attitudes toward insiders. Members had to be capable of aggression, but only on certain occasions. Neither community could simplify this problem by maintaining a posture of hostility toward all outsiders, although Taos came far closer to this than Namhalli. Namhalli had to maintain friendly relationships with neighboring communities and with the regional political organization, which had to be regarded both as an outside threat and as a means of protection. Taos evidently regarded other pueblos as possible sources of assistance, as in the Pueblo Revolt of 1680, but required no protection against outside political officials or, with some possible exceptions, against wars in which it was not directly involved. As part of a larger regional set of organizations, Namhalli probably affected its external conditions more than politically independent Taos.

In both communities protection against disease was largely an unsolved problem, although it may not have been as severe in Taos as in Namhalli. Both communities had to develop systematic explanations for the failure of the cultural tradition to predict outbreaks of disease. In dealing with disease, Namhalli, again in contrast to Taos, relied to some degree on external support. Many of the priestly functionaries who deal with the threat of disease have always come from outside the community.

Technological strains appear in virtually every domain of external relationship. Some problems—for example, fluctuations in the labor requirements of food plants—appear to be both generally insolvable and widely distributed among human cultures. Other problems—for example, detailed methods for handling maize— seem to be more localized. Because technological strains are located on the boundary between the cultural system and its surroundings, it is relatively easy to define expectations and to determine whether or not they are consistently met. At the same time, there is no really clear-cut dividing line between technological strains and other kinds of strains, and sometimes one cannot be sure that the problem is *from* the external world; it may equally well be a problem created *in* the external world by members of the cultural system. The growing of millet and maize poses specific problems for the people of Namhalli and Taos, and it is fairly obvious that such agriculture solves problems of food production. Why such solutions were chosen is not so clear. Presumably the problems created by this particular agricultural technology were more acceptable from a social and ideological viewpoint than the problems created by other available alternatives. We cannot, then, speak simply of coping with the outside world, for this coping must mobilize the organization's membership and its tradition. To manufacture and use a particular tool requires the efforts of several persons, or a particular kind of person, having a particular training. We cannot say whether the tool was chosen because the people were available, or whether people were sought and trained after the tool became available. Technological strains are in some sense more external to the organization than social strains, and insofar as survival is a technological matter, being a relationship between members and outside factors, technology has a certain priority.

SOCIAL STRAINS

Social strains are caused by the problem of predicting the behavior of other members of the organization. In one sense, social strains might properly be considered an aspect of technological strains, for if every member behaved as he should, there could be no social strain. Presumably, improper behavior occurs when technological strains interfere with the orderly process that assures the organization members who conform to its physical, biological, and social specifications. In other words, if there were no outside forces to interfere with the transmission of cultural traditions, there could be no occasions for unpredicted behavior among members, and hence no social strain.

Namhalli and Taos have both had problems with the division of labor, with the transmission of cultural materials to new members, and with the development of systems of authority and social control. Both solved their social problems by developing hierarchies of authority that depend on age, spiritual advancement, and sex, to name only the most important distinctions. Both communities were internally segmented, although the segmentations were different. In both communities an emphasis on harmony, easy social relationships, and equality was counterbalanced by an emphasis on authority and obedience, but here again there were important differences between the two.

A central feature of Namhalli's organization was the organization of duties, services, and rewards in terms of more or less ranked castes. Because the castes were hereditary, maintenance of caste membership rosters at constant levels was a source of strain. In addition, the highly specialized nature of certain castes meant that they could flourish in some ecological niches and not in others. A single village could not always maintain an arrangement of castes approaching the ideal either ideologically or in terms of efficiency. The hierarchy conceived on a regional level did not always exist at the local level; hence there were abundant opportunities for conflict concerning caste rankings. Naturally, the mere existence of multitudinous social segments within a small community, particularly in view of the differences in rank, occupation, and viewpoint among them, made it hard to coordinate effort.

Taos also had a marked system of stratification, although the only inheritable office was that of the Cacique, a special priest performing community-wide services. Social segments at Taos were demarcated in terms of (1) membership in a kiva group, which was expected of all adult men possessing certain ritual knowledge, (2) community services performed by these men, and (3) kiva headships conferred upon the oldest male member, who was also expected to be well-qualified, not just minimally qualified, in terms of the first two criteria. Theoretically it took many years to acquire advanced ritual knowledge and to perform enough community services to become eligible for kiva headships or the governor's office. To function ideally such a system requires just the right number of properly qualified men to be always available. In recent years the death of one kiva chief, followed very quickly by the death of his two logical successors, catapulted the next-ranking person, a young, inexperienced man, into a position of considerable power. During the same period, the weak and indecisive behavior of the hereditary Cacique left a power vacuum, and between youth on the one hand and indecision on the other, the traditional balance of authority was disrupted. Apparently, strains associated with succession to positions of authority, or for that matter with replacing any person by another, are both exceedingly common and exceedingly complex. In Namhalli the strain centers about selection on a hereditary basis; in Taos it centers about selection through training.

Another source of strain in both communities was the mere fact of hierarchy itself. At Taos, training, beyond a necessary minimum, depended upon personal interest, ability, and probably upon sibling order. Those with extensive kiva training and a record of political and religious service were most likely to be nominated as secular officials or members of their staffs. Those who failed to achieve even the minimum training required for religious initiation could never participate, or free themselves from relationships of dependency. Here, again, strain appears to be a two-edged sword. Those at the top and the bottom of the social hierarchy were bound to have different perceptions of reality, the man at the bottom being especially likely to encounter frustration and hardship. On the other hand, the reciprocal obligations of high man and low man were quite clear at both Taos and Namhalli, and actual conflict was likely to occur between persons of nearly equal rank, whose hierarchic obligations could not be sharply defined. Strain would appear to be inherent in both social distance and social nearness, probably because rules governing proper behavior tend to be qualitative whereas many differences between men—age and income, for example—tend to be quantitative. Respect for the aged means something different if the period involved is twenty minutes instead of twenty years.

In a general sense, recruitment and training of the membership was a problem in both communities. Taos depended almost entirely upon births and natural increase or decrease. Spouses brought in from outside generally possessed adequate domestic skills but lacked ritual knowledge. Namhalli obtained a comparatively larger proportion of its adult women from outside the community by means of a complex system of exchange, and also obtained male members by immigration. Lacking ties to other communities, Taos might be expected to have faced far greater problems in maintaining a population balance than Namhalli; but there is no evidence to this effect.

Namhalli appears to have had, if anything, greater strain than Taos over recruiting population. The accumulation of capital and the storage of grain were accomplished most efficiently by large joint families, yet, owing to the caprices of fortune, only a few such families could exist. Although paired with other villages in bride and groom exchanges, Namhalli appears to have had relatively more difficulty in locating appropriate brides and bridegrooms. The statistical implications of a preference for one's own sister's daughter as a bride suggest a good deal of disappointment and frustration. All in all, disruption of familial relationships appears to have been considerably more common in Namhalli than in Taos, although it must have been far less common in both communities when strong and effective authoritarian institutions were functioning.

Social strains appear to be caused mainly by the indoctrination and control of members, the specification of rights and duties, and the mobilization and recruitment of manpower. Such strains appear to stem from the biological characteristics of human beings, from failures in the transmission of information, and from the difficulties involved in having just the right number of the right kind of person in the right place at the right time. Human beings tend to grow old gradually instead of by culturally defined stages. Genetic and constitutional differences, together with differences in life history and family environment, guarantee that no two members of an organization will be identically socialized. The addition of social differentiation in terms of such things as caste and kiva membership, or social and economic hierarchies, leads to ever greater variations. The need to replace the very old or to maintain a full complement of role players invariably leads to difficulties and the possibility of conflict.

In both Taos and Namhalli there was a tendency to rank persons according to several different criteria. Even at basic levels of human interaction this can lead to considerable confusion. Both communities recognized the dominance of males over females and of the aged over the young—surely a simple and basic kind of classification defining a common form of the nuclear family. But even such a simple classification is disharmonic because a growing male child and his mother are bound to enter into conflict when at some point the male child attempts to exert dominance. In exerting his dominance, the male child places himself in a position of equality with his father, and this too, as Freud noted, may lead to conflict. A perfectly designed status system would be one in which such an inconsistency could never occur, in which power, wealth, intelligence, age, and good looks were all monopolized by the prince. For any particular society, it is theoretically possible to diagram those combinations and permutations of ranking criteria that place strains upon particular relationships. Thus, in the nuclear family, the most harmonious relationship should be that of father and daughter, followed by elder brother and younger sister.

IDEOLOGICAL STRAINS

It has been impossible to discuss technological and social strains without at the same time discussing what it is that people think they are doing. Ideological strains exist in the form of understandings about the nature of things and about derived plans or methods of procedure. In all organizations cognitive understandings exist concerning both the phenomenal world and the "real" world. The memberships of both Namhalli and Taos accept transcendental or ideological explanations of the universe that appear to be organized around those areas of life in which accurate prediction is difficult or impossible.

In Namhalli a concept of ultimate reality is available to interpret everything that happens in a perfectly functioning universe. Inasmuch as most persons lack the spiritual development needed to achieve perfect happiness in terms of that ultimate reality, and also discharge responsibilities to others in the phenomenal world, varying kinds of inconsistency exist in these sets of beliefs. The laws of karma can be thought of as an accommodation to this ideological strain, in that they state the kinds of moral behavior appropriate to one's level of spiritual development. Given the fact that different laws of karma are thought to operate for different roles, and that each person must play multiple roles, the rules of karma may themselves be in conflict with one another, not only as they affect intercaste behavior, but also as they affect choices made by any given person. For the citizen of Namhalli there are several paths to heaven. For any actor, therefore, the specific system of beliefs of other actors is partly unpredictable, even though all actors share a common reservoir of such beliefs. Namhalli villagers further recognize that where behavior is justified by neither dharma nor karma, divine punishments like crop failure or illness will follow. The indeterminacy of the outcomes of behavior—and the problems involved in determining which behavior is sinful and which is virtuous—requires strong authorities to make decisions for less sophisticated persons.

Taos ideology is composed of fewer elements, and involves augmentation rather than denial of the phenomenal world. It is consistent in this respect with less diversity and specialization among social roles and with lower economic productivity. More often the community as a whole is believed to suffer from wrong acts (which are interpreted as noncooperation or nonaccommodation). The village, acting in concert, must enlist the help of spirit powers in all phases of activities upon which the welfare of all depends, especially food-producing activities and transfer points in the life cycle; and to do so demands continual perfection of one's understandings through kiva training. Perfect harmony with transcendental powers requires harmony among men; conversely, the success of any enterprise requires scrupulous compliance with a complex body of ceremonial performances. Equal virtue is attainable by all men. Virtue is wisdom, however, and takes a long time to acquire. By the time one has reached a position of authority, one has as much power over subordinates as authorities in Namhalli have.

Taos has never created a theology or a class of theological specialists. One can hardly point to strains among the beliefs themselves. Classes of spirit powers tend to be discrete and to be brought into little relation to one another in men's minds. Taoseños are not interested in how the universe ought to operate in some ultimate reality. The "real" world embraces the phenomenal world; spirit beings act in concert with human beings, but only if the latter show the proper concern about their relationships with one another and with the spirits, and even then the hunter may not succeed, the farmer's crops may wither, and other signs of malfunctioning of the universe may appear. The basic strain in the belief system, therefore, is between the transcendental beliefs and the imperfect operation of natural (including human) forces.

Strain, we have asserted, grows out of the inevitably imperfect solutions to problems encountered in life. Each solution creates its own problems, which demand further solutions, in a kind of infinite regress. This is the principal internal dynamic of cultural systems. In the ideological domain of Namhalli, inconsistencies in the concept of dharma are often resolved by the concept of karma. Ambiguities created by the doctrine of karma appear to be handled by the idea of the Age of Kali and the concept of illusion. Although it is not always possible to arrive at the order in which particular beliefs developed, it is usually possible to state relationships among beliefs: if there is to be life after death, there must be a place to carry out life; if there is to be a heaven, there must be a source of persons to live in it.

Ideological strains appear to be of two general kinds: those that involve inconsistent beliefs (the acceptance of dharma and karma in Namhalli), and those that involve beliefs and consequent practices that do not have the predicted effect on the phenomenal world (the failure of harmony and good behavior to bring rain in either community). Presumably, the consistency of belief systems could be measured by detailed logical analysis. But determining which beliefs are true and which are false poses problems that can only be solved by assuming that the scientific method yields a closer approximation to reality than other methods. Such an assumption has its merits: theoretically, at least, the scientific observer is free from bias and can see things in some kind of perspective, thanks to his familiarity with a number of different organizations and cultural systems. On any other assumption the problem of identifying ideological strains becomes the irresolvable question of whose reality is real.

STRAIN SYSTEMS

The kinds of strain present in Namhalli and Taos appear to be linked together to form "strain systems." The complexity of even the simplest culture makes it extremely hard to isolate an entire system of related strains. The basic structure of strain systems is most easily explicated by considering first those aspects of the surroundings that create problems during the day-to-day operation of the cultural system. Such problems, which presumably are not susceptible to direct or technological coping, will presumably be handled by indirect solutions in the social and ideological spheres.

Granted the existence of linked systems of strains, there appear to be important differences in the over-all manner in which component strains are linked. In both Namhalli and Taos, strains appear to be linked by a hierarchy of authorities, in which each person has definite responsibilities toward persons both above and below him. Power is not exercised freely; it is severely curtailed by formal rules and by notions of harmony and balance. Villages in India, the eastern pueblos, and extensions of European communities (Spanish-American communities in New Mexico, for example) seem to depend upon a common denominator of overt controls exercised through family, religious, and political alignments. In Spanish-American society, the male family head's relationship to family members has a direct counterpart in the priest-follower and patron-employee relationships. These societies attempt to specify the proper way of doing things in vast detail. Where there are disagreements, they are supposed to be settled by appealing to persons higher up in the knowledge-authority hierarchy. Such persons do not legislate; they determine what should have been done in terms of the ideal model, and indicate what steps should be taken to restore perfect functioning.

Segmentary lineage systems appear to operate differently. Societies of this kind consist of a number of separate but equal unilineal kinship segments that have rights and duties distributed equally among them. There are few political controls external to these groups, and conflict between them must be regulated by discussion of jural and moral considerations or by mutual group interest—unity in the face of adversity, disunity in the face of good fortune. Where kinship is matrilineal or where matrilocal residence is a possibility, there appears to be recurrent tension stemming from divided loyalties in the avunculo-matrilineal and paternal role expectations of males. Residence norms and unilineal kin alignments in many of these cases appear to involve uneasy compromises with the fact of emotional ties. Such a situation is described by Fortes (1949, pp. 54–84). Whereas systems based upon strong authority relationships have rare but severe conflicts either around permanently organized cleavages or around unstable factions, segmentary societies appear to resolve conflicts at one level by developing conflicts at another level. Thus there is always a good deal of conflict, but it never lasts long enough to disrupt relationships permanently—and these relationships must, in any case, be resumed shortly in order to permit the carrying out of conflict at some other level.

Both these types of strain systems involve the presence of actual conflict and of formal political or social systems. In Egyptian villages, formality appears to be introduced by a strict code of manners involving mien, stereotyped gestures, and the tone, pitch, and melody of the voice. Conflict tends to be caused by inconsistent application of the code (Adams, 1957). Many systems—the Eskimo, for example—appear to seek ideological explanations of unpredictability that tend to rule out overt conflict except as a last resort. We do not yet have enough detailed descriptions of strain systems to permit meaningful classification, but different cultural systems can be seen to deal with strains between the cultural system and its environment in different ways. These different ways of handling unpredictability are presumably limited both in number and in the consequences they can have for the development of conflict in society. Finally, it can be assumed that man's strain toward consistency operates even in inconsistency, so that there is a tendency to combine strains of various kinds into a single system.

STRAIN, CONFLICT, AND SOCIAL THEORY

So far, our discussion has been based upon patterns of strain existing in Taos and Namhalli. This discussion has made it possible to suggest various kinds of strain and strain systems. Hopefully, the point has been made that strain systems are at least as real as political systems, economic systems, or social systems. All represent aspects of operating cultural systems. The concept of a strain system involves a model of cultural systems as characteristically working toward the solution of those aspects of their external relationships that tend to be unpredictable. Organizations are interpreted as problem-finding and problem-solving devices. Where problems are, in fact, insoluble, it is necessary to construct social and ideological systems that control or cover up the results of such insolubility. Strain systems (more properly "systems for handling strain") are functioning elements of an existing and ongoing system. Traditional functionalist explanations of human behavior have dealt with social systems and cultural systems without giving a great deal of attention to their external relationships or to change. External relationships were considered only in terms of homeostatic mechanisms. Organizations encountered problems, solved them, and returned to their normal resting positions. Such a viewpoint is basically a closed-system viewpoint; there can be no change because even external influences have a predictable and resolvable character. Such a closed system can exist only in a universe that is itself completely lawful or predictable. Where the universe is conceived to be a blooming, buzzing confusion, the theoretical model must be tinkered with. To put it another way, Durkheim (1912, p. 3) argued that human institutions founded upon error could not last: "If it is not founded on the nature of things, it will encounter resistances over which it will not triumph." But the average man, living in a rapidly changing world, can hardly regard the external forces that assail his community as a completely reliable "nature of things." Some institutions that worked in 1912 fail now, not because they were founded upon error, but because the nature of things changed to create new problems. Nature contains both order and disorder. Human organizations must adapt to both: to order by elaborating homeostatic mechanisms, to disorder by elaborating strain systems. The concept of strain has been perceived with varying degrees of clarity by different writers and

interpreted from different points of view. It was elaborated by
Simmel as early as 1908: "An absolutely centripetal and harmonious
group, a pure 'unification' (*Vereinigung*), not only is empirically
unreal, it could show no real life process" (1955, p. 15). Simmel
(pp. 16–17) points out that whereas unity means consensus and
concord in one sense, in another sense both concord and discord
contribute to organization. He describes such terms as discord and
opposition as being used at different levels of meaning to refer to
discord between individuals as well as to the disruption of organizations. In his enthusiasm for demonstrating (presumably in opposition to rural and traditional ideals of harmony) the notion that
conflict could be a good thing, Simmel is unable to carry the analysis of strain much farther.

Expositions of concepts of strain were introduced by Sapir in
1924 in his discussion of "genuine" and "spurious" cultures, and by
Bateson (1935) in his discussion of schismogenesis. Sapir recognized that some cultures offered a more predictable world than
others, but he used his discovery to criticize modern society and
failed to recognize that all cultures contain elements of strain or
"spuriousness." Bateson defined schismogenesis as "a process of
differentiation in the norms of individual behavior resulting from
cumulative interaction between individuals" (1936, p. 175). His
analysis is confined to intimate relationships between pairs of individuals, but it can equally be applied to categories or classes of
individuals, such as male and female, or older and younger. In
effect, Bateson suggests that conflict tends to occur as a result of
the gradual differentiation of norms. He also argues that unsatis-
factory or unexpected behavior may occur when the norms of (or
models for) conduct give differential satisfactions or impose di-
lemmas in role playing for which there are no clear-cut definitions
of appropriate behavior. Firth's account of a Tikopian man who
found himself to be a cognatic kinsman of the bride and an affinal
relative of the groom, Murphy's tale of "What makes Biboi run"
(1961), Beals's account of a younger brother's attempt to arrange
the marriage of his elder brother (1962, pp. 67–74), and some of
the accounts of conflict by Turner and by Mandelbaum indicate

the nature of this variety of strain. In all cases, conflicting role responsibilities necessitate personal choices and decisions that others
see as inconsistent with proper behavior in an integrated system.

Perhaps the view of strain and strain systems most similar to the
one advanced here is that of the Wilsons (1945), who speak of
strain as consisting of ordinary and of radical oppositions. Ordinary
oppositions "occur independently in different relations and divide
people over the occupation of the existing social positions—over
who is to be partner to whom, and over who, in particular, are to be
the leaders and who the subordinates—and over the application of
accepted laws, logical limitations, and conventions to particular
circumstances" (p. 125). The concept of "radical opposition" refers
in a more general way to circumstances surrounding rapid social
change. Because we tend to distinguish sharply between stable
characteristics of societies and the changes that result from their
changing relationships with their surroundings, our concept of
strain cannot be stretched to include radical oppositions, although
such an extension is logical. At points, radical opposition appears
almost to be synonymous with factionalist dispute: "Radical opposition is always muddled; that is to say, conflicting laws, contradictory concepts, and disharmonious conventions are supported
by the same people. Men are divided against themselves as well
as against their neighbours" (p. 127). A good part of what the
Wilsons describe as radical opposition is discussed here under the
heading of stress. We insist, as the Wilsons do, on the importance
of a distinction between strain, or ordinary opposition, and the
various forms of radical opposition.

The Wilsons to some extent, and other social theorists to an even
greater extent, have displayed a tendency to consider society apart
from its surroundings. A closed system, and by the same token a
static system, cannot have any meaningful relationships with an
environment, because the environment must be a constant. Society
conceived as consisting of relationships between people also ex-
cludes the idea that a society is related to an environment. Of
recent publications, the clearest statement of a viewpoint that
makes use of both environment (the "external system") and in-

ternal relationships (the "internal system") is that of Homans (1950). Our analysis bears many points of correspondence to Homans's theory, but ours does not depend upon the particular elements of group behavior (sentiment, activity, interaction, and norms) out of which his is built. By the external system, Homans means "the state of these elements and their interrelations, so far as it constitutes a solution . . . of the problem: How shall the group survive in its environment?" Subsequent complications of human relations with the cultural solutions observed at any given time— the internal system—are in large measure the operation of strains developed during interactions with the environment. Such inter- actions are clarified in the case studies, particularly in the rework- ing of Firth's ethnographic data on the Tikopian family. The con- cept of strain emerges again when Homans describes social dis- tance as a "source of conflict and failure of communication" (p. 274). Elsewhere Homans suggests that the application of new stresses, which disturb previous modes of coping, brings to the fore antagonisms for which there are no regulatory solutions. The result is disruptive conflict (p. 460).

In their discussion of strain, Parsons and Shils (1951) focus al- most exclusively upon the internal properties of organizations. Strain is defined as "the problems arising from the coexistence of different entities in the same system" (p. 224), but it also seems to exist between systems (p. 175): "Inconsistencies within the value system result in strain in the system of action, personal and social. . . . The original sources of strain [are] inherent in the na- ture of systems of action. This original source of strain lies in the fact that no fully integrated, internally consistent system of value orientations can be adequate to the functional needs of any con- crete system of action." Basically, we use the concept of strain in the same way that Parsons does, but we add to it the notion of problem solving and adaptation. Strain, then, becomes inconsis- tencies both within cultural systems and between the cultural sys- tem and its environment.

With the exception, then, of the Wilsons' extended discussion of strain as a part of their elaborated theory, and of Bateson's continued work with such concepts as schismogenesis and the "double-bind," strain and strain-like concepts have received relatively little attention in the anthropological literature.[1] These concepts cannot find a place in a static functional view of society. Must we then adopt the view that culture is, as Lowie remarked, "a thing of shreds and patches"? On the contrary, we join Clyde Kluckhohn (1948, p. 658) in extolling the "intricate interdependence of all segments of a people's life." Organizations exist because there are patterns of interaction, complementary and interrelated roles, networks of relationships, and the regular cooperative performance of tasks. Such harmony may be achieved either because everyone is performing the same task or because the various different tasks are parts of a whole; it is the shared understanding of that whole that creates the harmony. We very much favor the "replication of uniformity" and the "organization of diversity" (Wallace, 1961, p. 27), in particular where they can be shown to exist. And we repeat that what we deplore most strongly is the false implication that because organizations are organized, they must exhibit total functionality, perfect integration, or absolute organization.

Closely linked with the notion of perfectly functioning organizations as closed systems is the notion that such systems are maintained by conflict. One commonly advanced theory is that conflict stimulates apartness, and that this apartness creates cleavages among subgroups that in some unspecified way contribute to system functioning. This idea is brought up by Simmel in the argument that "The negative and dualistic elements play an entirely positive role in this more comprehensive picture [of the entire group], despite the destruction they may work on particular relations" (p. 17). According to Simmel, it is hostility and mutual repulsion that maintain caste systems in India. In marital relationships discord and controversy are organically connected with the elements that hold the group together (pp. 17–18). Gluckman (1955, p. 10) argues that a multiplicity of conflicts within a social

[1] Strain-like concepts are perhaps explicit in the work of Foster concerning peasant societies, and in Metzger (1960), Gulliver (1961), and Aberle (1950), to name a few.

system divides society "into a series of opposed groups with cross-cutting membership." Coser (1956, p. 80) suggests that social systems "tend to be sewn together by multiple and multiform conflicts."

Conflict, like sex, friendship, hunger, or "the power drive," may or may not contribute to the development or maintenance of social cleavages; it may or may not contribute to the well-being of those who do not participate in it. It is wrong to use the term conflict (as all of the above-cited authors do) to refer first to psychological distress, then to competition, and then to the war of all against all. We enjoy thinking about the individual Iroquois torn between his loyalty to his tribe and his loyalty to his clan, and we are fascinated by the marvelous latticework of conflicting loyalties existing among the Zuñi. To argue that the absence of conflict (if there really is such an absence) resulting from such an arrangement is due to the *presence* of conflict is merely a play upon homonyms. On Pukapuka an equally marvelous latticework involving conflicts of interests among territorial, kinship, and age-grade societies led to bloody battles on different occasions within each of the types of groups (Beaglehole and Beaglehole, 1938). In parts of South India, the two lowest-ranking social groups or castes are the "left-hand people" and the "right-hand people." There is a considerable enmity between the two groups, and it could be argued that this enmity helps maintain things as they are because the lower castes are too busy fighting each other to consider rebellion against the higher castes. Conceivably the conflict, by rendering the lower castes bellicose, encourages them to rebel and thus improves social circulation and helps maintain the social system.

A related point is made by Gluckman (1939, p. 168): "All social relationships have two aspects, one of fission, in which divergent interests tend to rupture the relationship, the other of fusion, by which the common ties in a system of social cohesion reconcile these divergent interests." Here again, confusion results from unsystematic mixing of levels. Such a statement is reasonable only if the parties involved in each relationship have the same motives or interests. For a relationship to exist, both parties must accept—

not necessarily enjoy or equally approve of—the inequities in gains and costs involved. Cohesive or divisive tendencies in the system as a whole are not adequate to explain particular relationships; they can only contribute to statistical probabilities. We cannot argue that the circumstances surrounding a particular relationship either determine or are determined by characteristics of the organization as a whole. Fights do not start because individual members wish to maintain the social system, or because the social system is momentarily more fissive than fusive. They start because certain persons, taking into account these factors and others, decide that an expression of opposition is appropriate. At a more subtle level, wherever we find interpersonal conflicts or fissive tendencies, we find forces at work that run counter to the maintenance of the social system, forces that involve ambiguity, incongruity, or imperfect communication.

The point is that no matter how well-designed a cultural system may be, no matter how clearly and thoroughly its members understand what behavior is appropriate at what time, outcomes are affected in some degree by individual decision. Because people are not perfectly socialized, because the world is not perfectly organized or predictable, human behavior and individual decision must always involve varying amounts of ambiguity, indeterminacy, or uncertainty. It is not necessary to argue that human beings gain free will and independence of action from some mystical entity such as a "soul" or a "personality"; all that is needed is to acknowledge that human beings receive messages from a variety of sources other than the particular cultural system within which they are operating at any given moment. Expressing such uncertainty by opposition toward one's neighbor or toward society in general may or may not help to maintain existing social alignments at various levels. It is worth remembering that only two-year-olds make friends with people by hitting them.

The argument that "all that is, is functional" is of value only in discussing closed and immutable systems. A discussion of changing systems does require the establishment of a "starting condition." We speak, then, of a relatively stable set of external conditions that pose a series of solvable and insolvable problems to the membership of the organization. These problems, particularly those vital to survival, are solved at varying technological, social, and ideological levels by the membership. In most cases, the solutions are slightly imperfect or create fresh problems that are also difficult to solve. Within the organization there come to be zones and areas where things are slightly less functional than they are in other areas. Quarrels and fights are more likely to occur in such zones than elsewhere. Things would be different if there were no such conflicts, but they cannot be regarded as a basic cause of group segmentation or as an essential element of social structure. At the same time, it cannot be argued that conflicts and potential conflicts within an organization are likely to cause its downfall.

Strain, whether it is expressed in social segmentation, in incompatibilities with the surroundings, or in inconsistencies within ideological structures, represents thin places in the fabric of social life. Whether the distribution of such weak spots will prove to be an advantage or a disadvantage to the further development of the organization depends upon other factors that develop in the surroundings. The emergence of new kinds of conflict, in particular of divisiveness and factionalist dispute, depends upon the development of a certain kind of new influences upon the character of the organization. It is these new influences that we define here as *stress*.

5. Stress

A stress differs from an external condition simply by virtue of being relatively new, and hence creating problems that cannot be solved by applying routine or traditional devices. Because every organization lives in the midst of a host of unsolved, half-solved, and indirectly solved problems, it is often difficult to discriminate between old stresses, which we call external conditions, and new stresses. At both Namhalli and Taos, the transition from normal external conditions to a condition of stress was fairly gradual, making it impossible to determine exactly when the two communities first encountered stress. However, in both villages it has been possible to establish with some accuracy the time at which major shifts in the application of problem-solving techniques began. It is our contention throughout this chapter that for both communities pervasive factionalism emerged because of an interaction between the particular pattern of stress affecting the communities and the characteristic pattern of strain.

STRESS AT NAMHALLI

At Namhalli rapid changes in the relationships between the village and the world around it began during the famine of 1876–78. A brigade of British troops was stationed a few miles away, and began to distribute food, clothing, and cattle. The presence of such a powerful, nurturant external authority was unprecedented. Equally unprecedented was the fact that this aid was distributed independently of the local power-prestige structure. In particular, the exclusive right of the local "big man" to mediate between the village and the outside world, and to superintend and organize distributions of food and clothing, was abrogated. The Headman of Namhalli, in addition to being denied his role as "father of the village," was grossly humiliated when his wife ran away with a British captain.

After the incidents of the famine years, the pattern of government action independent of village leadership continued. Pacification of the surrounding countryside was rapid, and by 1910 the hedge of thorns protecting the village no longer existed. Regulations and periodic inspections designed to encourage military preparedness among the villagers gave way before rules and regulations that would ultimately disarm the rural population. In 1903, when an epidemic of bubonic plague threatened the region, the government again intervened directly. Public health workers compelled everyone to move outside the village, poked ventilating holes in every house, and scrubbed almost everything and everybody with disinfectant. By the 1920's the environs of Namhalli were virtually free of armed bandits and raiders; the threat of famine had been eliminated; and all major epidemic diseases were under control. The famine of 1876–78 and the influenza epidemic of 1919 were the last great natural disasters that had any significant effect upon the population of the village.

Although the ordinary villager only gradually came to see that outside threats had been virtually eliminated, less and less use was made of the traditional defense mechanisms. The basically authoritarian structure of village leadership could no longer be justified as necessary for defending the village against attack. Insofar as government officials behaved with ever-increasing sympathy and benevolence, mediation by village officials between the village and the government must have seemed progressively less worthy of reward. Immediately following the famine the government constructed irrigation works and railroads, and instituted a land settlement in order to foster systematic taxation. The irrigation of land in Namhalli, originally undertaken for famine relief, appears to have served little immediate purpose, inasmuch as the famine had already reduced the population to the point where further food shortages were most unlikely. In Namhalli, people refused to plant the newly irrigated land or to pay taxes on it. Ultimately the government, working through the village Headman, compelled them to cultivate the land. Later, as population and grain prices increased, many persons were able to establish ownership of small patches of rice land. Except for a time during World War I, until well into the 1930's Namhalli produced a considerable surplus of food that could not readily be disposed of on a perennially glutted market.

The land settlement initiated during the 1880's replaced taxation in kind (a proportion of the harvested crop) with taxation in cash. Under the former system, both the government and the farmer wanted to maintain the market price of grain at the highest possible level. After the introduction of cash taxation, government policies consistently led to a reduction in the cash value of grain. Cash taxation in itself leads to such a reduction, because the farmer must sell his crop immediately after harvest to acquire sufficient cash to pay his land tax. Because all farmers are attempting to sell their grain at approximately the same time, there is a "harvest glut"; the price of grain falls, and the farmer must sell comparatively more grain in order to pay his taxes. The farmer's access to cash becomes limited, and what cash he is able to accumulate tends to go for taxes. This means that the farmer contributes to the urban economy, but is effectively excluded from participating in it as a buyer. Moreover, in South India new roads and railroads tended to level out "good" and "bad" years by permitting the economical transportation of grain from regions enjoying good crop production to those with poor crop production in any particular year. Thus, after the building of the railroads, the price of grain, and with it the ability of the village to participate in the urban economy, became dependent upon the world market and thus beyond the control of the village.

The land settlement, cash taxation, and improved transportation had several further effects. First, the role of the Headman, who had allotted land according to each farmer's needs at the time of the New Year festival, was altered; the Headman became a large landholder, and others acquired ownership of the land they were actually farming. The need to pay taxes on large acreages of land, which could not be farmed because of the persistent labor shortages, made it impossible for the Headman to retain his claim to the lands he had acquired under the land settlement. Moreover, the Headman during the period immediately after the land settlement wanted to establish himself as a businessman rather than as a farmer. What cash he had he poured into unsuccessful businesses in a nearby town, and in time his lands were forfeited to the government for nonpayment of taxes. Had the Headman chosen to retain his lands at all costs, as the headmen of other neighboring villages did, the history of the village might well have been different. As the government acquired large acreages by tax default, it had to lease or give away the lands to anyone who would pay the taxes on them. Thus, the obvious effect of successive government programs upon Namhalli was to reduce the landholdings of the wealthy and to increase the landholdings of the poor. By the 1920's Namhalli was a village of more or less equal small farmers that had no significant hierarchy of wealth or influence. It is very likely that this drift toward an egalitarian distribution of landholdings had a strong ecological basis. The village has never had large acreages of irrigated land, and the surplus of food production over food consumption may well have been too small to support a landlord-tenant or owner-servant type of agricultural economy.

Sometime between the years of the famine and 1900, the Headman and the Accountant, the two major officials of the village, were placed on governmental salaries. In time they ceased to be natural leaders, and became government officials firmly caught in a "Foreman's Dilemma" between those under them and those above them. Immediately after 1910, two Headmen in succession were punished and removed from office for misappropriating village funds despite the fact that their activities were no different from those of previous Headmen. Descendants of the original Headman remained in office until 1953 with progressively declining status. In 1953 a Headman from a different family line and a different jati was appointed.

Legislation and governmental policies created an increasingly direct relationship between the individual villager and government officials. Social legislation concerning the age of marriage, the relationships between jatis, and the inheritance of property undermined the authority of caste and village pancayats, or village councils. The government showed its opposition to the caste system by offering free land, free housing, educational scholarships, and other forms of assistance to members of the lowest-ranking jatis. The high-ranking Brahmin jati, represented by the Village Accountant, was systematically denied educational privileges and employment opportunities. The introduction of Western legal processes, in particular the court of law, made it possible to circumvent the traditional authorities, many of whom no longer enjoyed official governmental support. To the extent that the law courts enforced Western-style laws on inheritance, marriage, and jati interrelationships, it became harder and more dangerous for village officials and village councils to uphold traditional law and practice, since their adverse rulings could be appealed to the law courts.

In 1900 Bangalore was little more than a military encampment, and people from Namhalli avoided entering it for fear of being manhandled by Muslim camp followers or English soldiers. By 1953 the average citizen of Namhalli felt deprived if he did not go to the movies in the city at least once a month. Although during much of the period between 1900 and 1953, the villager was excluded from urban life by a lack of cash, urban influences created a number of new circumstances within the village. Very early, urban manufactured goods drove many of Namhalli's craft specialists out of business. As these specialists turned increasingly to agriculture to make a living, the range of occupational diversity within the village decreased. Later, as improved education made it possible for people from Namhalli to find urban employment, the range of occupational diversity within the village began to increase again.

Urban contacts led to the introduction of new modes of dress, new crops, new values, and new models for behavior, but not to a new system of values. The city offered many disparate and unrelated value systems that had no obvious application to village life. The city included British soldiers, Christian missionaries, urban Hindus and Muslims, lower-class working men, and middle-class schoolteachers and factory employees. Eventually the city acquired or developed new, synthetic value systems representing "modern," "modern Hindu," and "modern Indian" points of view. As urban influences increased, a wider range of values and practices could be justified in terms of an ever-increasing number of urban reference groups.

Regardless of whether the attractions of the city lay in the hedonistic life of the urban sophisticate or the ascetic but highly political implications of Gandhian thought, the common coin needed to play the urban game was money. Traditionally, a man's wealth was computed in terms of the size of his manure heap and the amount of grain in his storage bins; under urban influence a man's importance began to be computed in terms of his cash income. Except during the rather rare periods when the price of grain was high, cash, whether for educating one's children or for visiting urban houses of prostitution, was difficult to obtain. The city created new needs for medical care, stylish clothing, cinema attendance, dietary improvement, education, metal cooking utensils, and metal farm implements. Most of these needs could not be satisfied.

The impact of a long-continued population increase was slow in making itself felt, but it can clearly be traced to the pacification of the region, to the control of epidemic diseases, to the maintenance of a relatively stable economy, and to the breakdown of traditional methods of population control. Ironically, the increases in population at Namhalli were the result of more favorable living conditions, but the increased population could not be fully employed within the village, and by 1953 may well have been pressing heavily upon village resources. For example, the extent of the cultivated lands surrounding Namhalli has increased almost every year, largely at the expense of pasture lands. Very probably the capacity to manure village lands has decreased as supplies of fodder and numbers of livestock have decreased. It is likely that with increasing population there was a decrease in the yield per acre and perhaps in the total yield of village lands. Few could move out of the village because of population pressure throughout the region. Hence, one effect of the new stress upon Namhalli was to confine an ever-increasing population within an environment that could not be exploited much more with the techniques at hand. Population control was made difficult or impossible by a legal system that forbade such traditional means as infanticide, regulation of marriage, or expulsion from the community, and by a shortage of cash that made impossible the large-scale application of modern birth-control techniques.

In short, after the famine of 1876–78 a set of problems emerged that were not subject to solution by traditional means. The coming of the British, the development of the city of Bangalore, and the introduction of roads, railroads, and public health measures are sufficiently interrelated to be regarded as in some sense a single influence upon the village. At the same time, to say that this period of stress was a period of acculturation, urbanization, or modernization hardly does justice to the complexity of the outside forces that impinged upon Namhalli. In the following section, a similar series of events occurring in Taos will be described. We shall then consider the basic elements of two stress situations that are very different in detail, but very similar in their effects.

STRESS IN TAOS

In 1680 the eastern pueblos revolted against Spanish dominion. They retained independence until 1693, when the Spanish successfully reconquered them. The handling of new stresses that began about 1700 led to the establishment of a relatively stable state that lasted until the middle of the nineteenth century. Although coercive measures must have been required following the reconquests, a pattern of peaceful and permissive relations soon developed. By this time Taoseños had added a number of European and Mexican cereals, fruit, and livestock, as well as new

methods of irrigation and cultivation, to their agricultural technology, and horse and ox carts had improved their transportation.[1]

Both the Indian and the Mexican-Spanish populations remained
small, and there was little competition for agricultural land. During the eighteenth century the population of Taos and other
pueblos was drastically reduced. Newly introduced communicable
diseases took their toll, and many disaffected Indians moved volun-
tarily into Hispanic settlements. The Spanish did encroach upon
Taos's lands during the late eighteenth century, but there is no
documentary evidence of conflict. A rough calculation of population density shows that the Indians' sources of livelihood were not
threatened at that time.

Our analysis of stress at Taos can start, then, with changes in
external circumstances beginning in the mid-nineteenth century.
From that time on, the loss of land as a result of encroachment by
both Hispanic- and Anglo-Americans, the stabilizing of resources
within defined limits, and the beginning of a steady growth in
population created serious and fundamental conflicts. The basis
upon which land disputes were finally resolved in the 1930's, and
the paternalistic relations between Anglo officials and the Indians,
were the principal stresses to which the pueblo was subjected. The
major changes in Taos have been the establishment of fixed boundaries (the generous ones originally established during the Mexican
grant period) and a rising population. The increase in population
was facilitated by the establishment of free medical and hospital
care, which greatly reduced the rate of infant mortality.[2]

By the time land disputes were finally adjudicated in Taos, the
pueblo had laid claim to 4800 acres of arable land, which, since it
was a ward of the government, were inalienable. That hunting and

[1] The principal sources for the Spanish colonization and consolidation of social
and technical innovations among the eastern pueblos, and for the stabilizing
of the environment and relations among these groups, are: Bolton, 1916; Espinosa, 1940; Hackett and Shelby, 1942; Hammond, 1926; Hammond and Rey,
1927 and 1929; Hodge, Hammond, and Rey, 1945; Scholes, 1930, 1935, and
1942; and Winship, 1896. The literature pertaining to this period, between
1540 and 1804, has been ably analyzed by Edward Dozier, 1962.
[2] Successful adaptation in the latter respect is reflected in an increase from 401
to 913 during the period from 1890 to 1947. See Siegel, 1949, p. 567.

farming could no longer be carried out within the fluctuating limits of an earlier day presented the pueblo authorities with a direct and obvious problem of cultural continuity. But the nature of the threat—how it would affect traditional problem solving—was much less obvious. If movement and indigenous control could at this time be arbitrarily constrained in a certain way, it might as capriciously be further reduced at some other time. Taoseños would never know when further encroachments might be made, nor on what outside factors such encroachments might depend. Ideological support of Taos institutions is traditionally based on man-land-nature relations, and it requires the physical presence of citizens within the community walls whenever they are not farming or hunting or visiting other pueblos for ritual events. The interweaving of productive tasks with sacred beliefs and actions tended to confer upon the land itself a sacred value. The pueblo leaders had no precise idea of the amount of land needed in relation to total population. Hence they could not clearly perceive when the territorial range necessary to cope with an increase in population would threaten the survival of the pueblo in terms of the life goals stressed in the training of new members. In a subtle way, the closed society tended to interfere with the traditional redistribution of resources among families as their sizes waxed and waned in successive generations. Thus changed environmental conditions, in a quite unforeseen manner, created a new criterion of wealth differences as a principle governing access to rank.

For analytic purposes it is possible to distinguish between the stresses of enclosure and population pressure, although they act upon each other. Each derives from separate, specific developments external to the group. Enclosure, we have seen, involves a long history of dispute over land rights, first between Hispaños and Indians, and subsequently among Hispaños, Anglos, and Indians. Population pressure seems to be the result of a set of conditions, including acquired immunity to certain contagious diseases, changes in the availability and use of medical services, and decreasing use of traditional birth-control practices. It is virtually impossible to obtain hard data on these conditions. When Coronado first visited Taos shortly after 1540, he estimated that the pueblo had a population of close to 3,000. This was perhaps somewhat exaggerated, but recent investigations at neighboring Picuris,[3] for which Coronado gave a similar estimate, indicate that the pueblo had more than 2,000 inhabitants. We have no population figures at all for the three centuries following Coronado. In 1890, however, a supplement to the eleventh U.S. Census gave a total of 401 persons. Five subsequent readings through 1947, when Bernard J. Siegel first undertook field work in the area, reveal a cumulative increase within this sixty-year period of about 125 per cent, to over 900 inhabitants (Siegel, 1949, p. 567). At present (1965), the population has grown to over 1,200.

There is no evidence, archeological or historical, from before 1540 to the end of the nineteenth century, that offers any insights into Taos population dynamics. We do not know, for example, whether the figure cited by Coronado represents a fairly stable population over a period of time, whether there had been prior growth or fluctuations in gross numbers, what the growth rates were, or how they were related to traditional birth-control methods. It is clear only that a dramatic decrease occurred, that it was closely associated with the introduction of new diseases, and that it may have come in part from defections to the Spanish settlements (Dozier, 1954).

Population increase and the fixing of boundaries have in fact operated as a single set of interrelated stresses, inasmuch as changes in the one affect the anxiety aroused by the other. In recent times it has been estimated that, given the prevailing food-producing technology and tastes, and discounting preferences for competing modes of livelihood, the amount and nature of the available arable soil and the short growing season would between them allow less than half the population to wrest a living from the land. All families are at least part-time gardeners, but an increasing number seek other employment. A few men in the past generation

---

[3] Systematic digging at Picuris was started in 1961 by Dr. Herbert Dick. It has been remarkably successful in revealing the original site and extent of the original settlement.

have been successful small-scale entrepreneurs. Two have opened curio stores catering to the tourist trade and one has introduced a much-needed grocery store. Most of the others work for wages outside the pueblo. The implications of this loss of manpower within the pueblo we shall consider shortly.

The pressure on resources is itself the result of a third precipitating stress in the pueblo environment, namely, the transfer of political control from the Mexican authorities to the American. One effect of this transfer has been a steady increase in Anglo settlers, notably civil servants, merchants, traders, teachers, artists, and builders. The town of Taos, partly Hispanic but predominantly Anglo, was a mere hamlet at the turn of the century. It is now a large village of almost 2,500.

The Anglos that flowed into the Taos area included an ever-increasing number of tourists. Occasionally, some tourists, through personal contacts, visited in the homes of Indians, but generally they simply wandered about at random. Gradually the villagers were alerted that the kiva areas and the path leading to the sacred lake were to be off-limits to the tourists. But because the situation was vague and unpredictable, the Indians were on the whole very worried about the proper procedure for handling it. The problem became chronic, but it was especially acute during large ceremonials that were traditionally open to the public (in an earlier day this had meant visiting Indian friends and Spanish-American compadres). As long as outsiders were defined as "casual visitors," influential persons might argue for their exclusion from the walled area. Later, when they were defined as "tourists," the social environment was perceived in a rather new way. Screening and handling tourists was destined to affect different Indian officials in different ways.

Another important outside agent of change is the United Pueblo Agency in Albuquerque, which mediates Washington's Indian policy and helps adjudicate disputes that local pueblo authorities cannot effectively handle. The Agency is a double-edged sword so far as the Indians are concerned. It provides special privileges, such as free agricultural aid (in the form of a special farm teacher), education, and hospital care; and it provides funds for dams, wells, and concrete irrigation ditches. But the Spanish, who see their manner of life as posing problems very similar to those of the Indians, resent having to pay for these services, either directly or by taxation; and their relations with the Indians, already embittered by a century of land disputes, have deteriorated further as a result of this resentment.

The establishment of new enterprises by Anglos, particularly in the town of Taos, and the surge of housebuilding by settlers and summer residents, created jobs for Taos Indians. It also provided a model for innovation within the pueblo itself. Both wage labor (with its new prescriptions for behavior) and entrepreneurship were alien to Taos in the mid-nineteenth century. By 1925 a few Indians were working in a variety of skilled and unskilled capacities. A quarter-century later some thirty men and fifteen women were working as domestics and cleaning women in private Anglo establishments (Siegel, 1949, p. 569). Today this number has increased at least threefold. Several men have opened stores and factories to serve local needs and to take advantage of the tourist trade. All these new jobs now constitute an important aspect of the environment. They offer alternatives to pueblo productivity, and their disappearance would create a substantial dislocation in pueblo life. Few, if any, Taoseños see these new job resources as likely to promote or hinder the future growth of their pueblo— nor, indeed, are they in a position to exert much control over external economic developments. On the other hand, Taoseños have not been confronted with the complexities of market conditions far from their settlement. They do not produce for export; even the small moccasin factory makes most of its sales locally.

Employment outside the pueblo involves forms of interaction and concepts of work and responsibility that are not only different from traditional work habits but also often in conflict with them. A person may choose either to live according to traditional regulation in the pueblo, or to live by two sets of rules. If he decides, sometime around puberty, to supplement farming with non-pueblo employment, he must conform part of the time to Anglo rules.

Punctuality, a workday consisting of a specific number of hours, and holidays geared to an alien calendar may interfere with pueblo expectations and demands. When this occurs, the appropriate choice is clear enough in theory: one simply leaves the job when, and for as long as, one is needed. But penalties, in the form of a loss in pay, a loss of pleasurable contacts, or even loss of the job itself, often tempt one to act otherwise. If this lack of obedience to the pueblo became widespread—if members were not readily available when summoned or if they weakened the power of the group by their friendliness with outsiders—families and ceremonial societies would not be able to perform their tasks effectively. Interpersonal conduct, the rendering of services, and participation in activities of central concern to the village must be controlled in order to ensure the least amount of damage to pueblo life and to make possible the effective punishment of offenders. For some, therefore, the new demands and complications of outside contacts provide excuses for avoiding irksome obligations; for others, they subvert rank privileges and community welfare.

Of all the environmental changes affecting relatively isolated groups, probably the least studied has been the building of roads. Concluding a brilliant historical analysis of a little-known but important Maya uprising and nativistic movement in Yucatan during the nineteenth century, Nelson Reed (1964) describes factors that weakened commitment to the movement. Belief in an ultimately successful opposition to the Spanish Ladinos required isolation from contending forces. "The fact that you can take a bus to Phillipe Carrillo Puerto at all," he says, "and make the journey in a few hours instead of five days, that a sick man can be driven to a doctor in Peto instead of dying, that food can be brought in during a bad year for the corn, that a starving farmer can move one hundred miles in search of work—these things tell part of the story" (p. 274). The broad plains to the east of Taos have long encouraged travel and contact with other tribes. This is a sparsely inhabited area, however, so that early communication with other Indian groups, even after the introduction of the horse, involved little necessity for adapting quickly to changing circumstances. The principal lines of movement followed valleys, passes, and stream beds to the north, south, and southwest. The advent of automobiles and trucks led to the construction of a major paved highway north from Santa Fe, and within the last two generations a network of good roads has come to provide quick transportation to centers of employment previously remote from the pueblo. It has also, of course, facilitated visiting between Taos and other pueblos, where people had long been accustomed to spending many hours attending ceremonials.

For Taos citizens, the arrival of modern transportation has meant basically two things: increased interaction with local outsiders and easier access to places distant from the pueblo. Taoseños have had to adapt themselves, at home, to a rapidly increasing number of new arrivals in their immediate vicinity. This is both a challenge and a threat, the challenge being to make use of the increased resources. The threat, which increases daily, is to the maintenance of cultural integrity. Before Spanish and Anglo contacts became habitual, the hostilities generated by the closed society within the pueblo could find outlet, for example, in moving and establishing a new settlement. Some families might simply build homes farther from the nucleated center. Many moved annually to summer homes and thus lessened the interaction within the group. The rapid encirclement of the settlement, together with the fixing of pueblo boundaries and increased population density, rather suddenly confronted Taos leadership with the problem of cultural survival. Leisurely contemplation of the choices provided by outside forces was no longer possible.

A second consequence of good modern transportation was the close linkage of Taos with population centers to the south and west. Although hostile attitudes toward the Spanish have kept dissidents from moving into neighboring Spanish villages, the attraction of life in the larger towns and cities has been strong. So far, relatively few persons have actually left, but friendships with Anglos are becoming more frequent, and the temptations are great, especially for the young. The recent emphasis in Indian secondary schools on vocational training has meant new jobs for some in enterprises in the Southwest and elsewhere. A change in Indian policy during the 1950's, by which Indians were urged to resettle in urban areas throughout the country, had a marked influence, particularly on the young.

The extent to which these developments are perceived and reacted to as environmental changes depends on the strains that exist within the pueblo social system. Early socialization establishing an intense commitment to village life can vitiate the alternatives that others see.[4] Even when a person feels frustrated about attaining pueblo goals, and has the techniques (such as language and craft skills) needed to settle in an urban center, he may be unable to comprehend that a change is possible. It should also be noted that whereas in an earlier day people could not move back and forth between different kinds of communities, today they can. A move to Santa Fe, Albuquerque, or even Oakland is not irrevocable. One may return to the pueblo. For the village this implies a certain indeterminacy of membership that did not exist previously.

A further influence on pueblo social life is the presence of Anglo nurses hired by the Bureau of Indian Affairs to work in the clinic, which, like the school, is located within the walls of the village. The nurses have apparently not been obliged to compete with traditional curers, since there have been few medicine men in recent Taos history, but their presence day in and day out within

---

[4] The early learning processes of males and females are quite different in Taos. Young girls are trained almost solely to maintain the home. This domesticity frees youths and men for the considerable time they spend in learning and performing rituals. Women learn only certain roles in ceremonial dances, and are expected to participate in these when called upon, but are ignorant of the symbolism that expresses the particular goals of the group. They learn that the kivas and the sacred Blue Lake must be defended against curious outsiders, but they do not know the connotations such things actually have in the ideology of the group. Being in this sense irrationally committed to cultural values, they may be even more stringent and indiscriminate than the men in trying to keep strangers from learning about them. Some women have domestic jobs for varying periods outside the pueblo, but they are told only what is needed for the job. It is interesting to note, therefore, that whereas men tend to learn much more about the outside world, *traditional understandings* are transmitted anew to each generation by the important role of women in early socialization.

the community has been looked on as a more subtle kind of threat: they peddle a different belief system. Since the Indians, particularly the women and children, make considerable use of medical services, there is a certain ambiguity in their attitude toward the nurses. They would like to limit their relationships with the nurses to the purposes for which they visit the clinic. The nurses, on the other hand, often see the need for home visits. On such occasions, what the nurse sees as environmentally important to the patient's treatment may seem irrelevant to the patient himself, and may arouse anxieties about revealing pueblo secrets. Two very real results of the introduction of Western medicine and its practitioners in the pueblo are the reduction of infant mortality and the elimination of certain epidemic diseases. Obviously, this saving of lives helps to increase the population.

Of all the innovations introduced by the Indian Bureau, the construction of schools might conceivably have had the greatest impact. For the children of European immigrants, there is no question that schools, teachers, and native-born fellow students do much to hasten the process of assimilation. For native-born Indians, however, the classroom often serves to emphasize their inferior status, as it has for Mexican-Americans, often simply by the very curriculum, which administrators considered realistically appropriate to their aspirations. It is explicitly directed toward craft, semiskilled, or skilled employment. It does not prepare students for college education or professional training, but it does assume that an increasing number of young men and women will seek jobs outside the pueblo. In this vein, government funds are also available for apprenticeships in Santa Fe and Albuquerque leading to jobs as beauty parlor operators, sheetmetal workers, and the like.

Until very recently, Indian schools were set apart from public schools, so that there was no interaction with children from alien backgrounds.[5] Moreover, unlike most other pueblos, whose chil-

[5] Integration of the public schools in recent years has affected Indians as well as Negroes. Increasingly, Indian children attend schools in the town of Taos predominantly attended by the Spanish majority. No study has yet been made of the implications of this change for pueblo life.

dren were sent to boarding schools in Santa Fe and Albuquerque, Taos had its own secondary as well as primary schools. In other words, children could complete their education without ever leaving the village. Even so, new ideas were transmitted randomly and unpredictably in the classroom, to the alarm of parents and traditional authorities who have no control over what is taught or how it is taught. New knowledge can and subtly does conflict with traditional understandings. For the more conservative members, Anglo formal education causes grave anxiety. Only by ensuring that the young are committed at a critical age to an identity with the Taos Way can they cope with the potential threat such education poses to their control.[6]

For most of this period of formal education pueblo authorities were able to withdraw children from school at a certain age for a year and a half of training in the kivas. As far as the Council is concerned, the school is kept at arm's length, so to speak. Teachers and principals are appointed and curricula approved in Albuquerque, and parents do not encourage achievement of the goals that the school promotes. Indeed, Taos authorities have little understanding of the operation of schools. When a young Indian who had received an excellent higher education became principal of the pueblo school, he was urged to appoint certain teachers chosen by local officials and to adjust the school program to the religious calendar. Because all personnel, including himself, were appointed by the Indian Bureau, he could resist the pressure, but only at the cost of creating further anxiety and potential conflict. The young principal lacked the legitimate qualifications for power in Taos terms, yet was in a position to withstand the pressure of local powerholders. What was to be made of such a man? As a well educated man, in the Anglo sense, his standing in the community was made more ambiguous by his serving at the same time as secretary to the Council and translator for agents of the Indian Bureau.

The G.I. Bill of Rights provided a very special opportunity for

[6] The confusion on this point is reflected in the demands that past governors and kiva chiefs have made upon the school principal for relaxation of school controls upon students—as if the principal had the power to decide these matters.

returning Taos war veterans—and a special problem for the community—by making available education beyond the secondary school level. Although none of the veterans went to college, either because of lack of motivation or because of insufficient preparation, several did study with local artists in the Anglo town of Taos. Under these circumstances pueblo authorities had virtually no control over the communication that took place during the course of closely supervised and intimate work between teacher and student. Some artists were surprised at the technical competence of beginning Indian students, and wondered how and where they had gained such proficiency. Despite a reluctance to talk about the matter, a few young men did relate their work and interest to kiva practices. Other confidences were exchanged as friendships developed. One can appreciate the concern this caused the secular and religious authorities, and why they tried to put a stop to instruction outside the pueblo.

STRESS

In its dealings with its surroundings every organization faces external conditions and stresses. Although the distinction between an external condition and a stress is not *always* evident, all forces sufficiently strong to cause unprecedented changes in the boundary relationships of an organization can be regarded as stresses. In effect, then, stresses may be defined as unprecedented events or as problems that cannot be handled by ordinary means. In the sense that a person can be injured without knowing what hit him, an organization can endure stress without recognizing its existence or without recognizing it as stress. Perceived threats are very different in their effects from other kinds of stresses, and of course there can be perceived threats—mysterious black mountain lions prowling suburbia—where no actual stress exists. The fact that stress can be present and not perceived, or perceived but not present, means that the description of stresses applied to organizations is considerably more complicated than laboratory stimulus-response experiments might lead one to believe. In real life, one does not encounter absolutely unperceived stresses or completely unsupported perceptions, but neither does one encounter stimuli that are perfectly perceived.

On the surface, the stresses that confronted both Taos and Namhalli are wholly familiar. Both communities were exposed to modern influences and to relatively benevolent governmental forces. Both lost elements of their traditional political and legal autonomy, and encountered population problems, cash and wage-labor economies, schools, new value systems, and so on. But a catalogue of specific new influences tells us little about the kind of problem that had to be solved. So far as the village itself is concerned, in Namhalli and Taos it does not really matter if new influences stem from the cinema, from urban contacts, or from schools. What matters is that a value conflict occurs. If motion pictures and schools pose problems of a different kind, even this difference should be made evident in a comparison of communities that have schools with those that do not. The more important concern is with the type of stress encountered rather than with its source. Again, one might suppose that because the people of Taos lived in the same region as the Navaho and the Apache, they would undergo the same stresses. In fact, the Navaho and the Apache engaged in violent wars, whereas the influences on the Taoseños were largely nonmilitary. Because Namhalli is similar to other Indian villages in many ways, it might be assumed that its acculturative experiences were roughly the same as those of all other Indian villages; but not all such villages experienced famines at the time Namhalli did, and not all such villages received assistance from a benevolent government. It is convenient to speak of Westernization or modernization, but such general concepts have little value in a discussion of particular communities or organizations. If we want to know and understand what happens to some particular organization, we must be able to describe with some precision the stresses affecting that organization.

In defining a stress, we must first ask how easily its presence and its true character may be detected. For both Namhalli and Taos, the presence of a new influence was obvious, but the true character of the new influence was very difficult to detect. In Namhalli the possibility that famine relief measures and medical care would result in a serious population increase was virtually inconceivable when the measures were introduced. The experts themselves were shortsighted, and it was not until the late 1930's that writers on rural Mysore began to worry about overpopulation. Even when the census returns showed a consistent pattern of increase, experts persisted in their traditional concern about underpopulation. The histories of both Taos and Namhalli involve an almost parallel series of benefits—protection, food, generous gifts of land, and medical care. No one dreamed that the end result would be to limit territorial resources while population increased.

The panorama of visible stress was only the top of the iceberg, for most of the influences affecting both communities were subtle and beyond easy comprehension. Both communities faced problems of adjustment, but in neither was there any full comprehension of just what was involved. A problem was known to exist, but no one knew what it was. Visibility is a matter of degree, and should be describable in quantitative terms, but any such description would require far more carefully recorded history than is available for either Taos or Namhalli. The most that can be said is that visibility was low in both cases.

Perception of the character of the stress was also made difficult by the fact that events occurred in both communities in an unpredictable fashion, as part of a highly complicated over-all problem. Because both Taos and Namhalli knew little about the rest of the world, such events as famines, fluctuations in market prices, epidemics, and world wars seemed even more random to them than was actually the case. Here, in developing techniques for coping with the new problem, both communities were handicapped by an inability to perceive very many regularities. Who, at Taos, for example, could perceive that performance of the very ceremonies condemned by missionaries would lead to an invasion of tourists who appeared, on the whole, to approve of the ceremonies? At Namhalli, after everyone had adapted to machine-made cloth, what sense was there is suddenly demanding that everyone wear handmade cloth?

Such apparent randomness was accentuated by the very complexity of the new influence. In accepting the presence of American soldiers during World War II, Taoseños accepted tourists, artists, highways, wage labor, and all the other problems accompanying the urbanization and industrialization that were part of their transition to the status of enclave community. When people in Namhalli accepted gifts of cattle and clothing from the British soldiers, they could not have imagined that sixty years later one of them would be employed full time as a "mosquito inspector" or that another would be a "coil winder." For both communities, the stress was so complex that there was no possibility of developing a single uniform solution to the whole situation.

Traditionally, Namhalli and Taos had been almost independent. Namhalli, to be sure, was subject to periodic taxation and was inextricably linked to neighboring communities. For both, the stress situation involved a gradual reduction of available alternatives. In Namhalli, the choice of alternative means of action was limited both by time and by political and economic force. At the time of the famine, people were scarcely in a position to refuse government largesse or to demand that it be administered by village leadership. Flight or emigration as a means of avoiding government control was possible only for a few. Even if people had wished to maintain their traditional high rate of mortality in order to prevent population growth, they could not have done so because the epidemic diseases that maintained the rate were largely eliminated without their knowledge. The weakening of traditional and authoritarian sanctions made it impossible to apply such traditional means of population control as increasing the age differential between brides and grooms or increasing bride and groom prices. Other traditional alternatives—armed revolt, refusal to sell grain or pay taxes, even the beating up of minor government officials—also became impossible.

In Taos, a similar series of constraints operated, and the amount of government interference was far greater. Taos had more autonomy to lose than Namhalli, and it received far more governmental assistance and control. Taoseños also had to learn how to entertain large numbers of tourists and how to deal with neighbors who had a radically different way of living. Namhalli, despite considerable experience with foreigners, never endured the loss of privacy suffered by Taos. In defining constraint, a problem arises when, as in the control of disease, a stress has the effect of removing older constraints. From the standpoint of things as they are, or were, such removal may also be regarded as constraining in the sense that there is a compulsion to do things that had not been done previously. We can define constraint, then, as either a multiplication *or* a reduction in the alternatives available. Because such changes in the distribution of alternatives can have extremely important effects upon organizational activity, knowing exactly what the available alternatives are—e.g., wage labor, agriculture, migration—may be more important than knowing how many of them there are. Broadly speaking, it appears that the patterns of constraint applied to both Namhalli and Taos had the effect of increasing the alternatives available to individuals, but of decreasing the alternatives available to the communities as a whole.

In neither Taos nor Namhalli did stress affect all members of the community equally. Changing external conditions caused losses to some, particularly the leadership, but permitted real gains for others. The differential impact of a stress upon the members of an organization can be called selectivity. In the case of Namhalli, the stress made the role of village officers difficult, raised the status of the lower castes, and improved the economic status of the artisan caste, but reduced the economic status of the weaver caste. Similarly, the access of some members of the Taos community to wage labor, to military service, and to the G.I. Bill of Rights created problems for those who claimed status on traditional grounds.

A complex stress, such as a flood or a volcanic eruption, which ends almost as soon as it has begun, may trigger a series of social changes, as Typhoon Ophelia did in 1960 on Ulithi in the Caroline Islands (Lessa, 1964). As Lessa suggests, such changes are not so much the result of the disaster as of other forces. When a complex stress is applied steadily over a long period of time, attempts to cope with it must also be maintained. Change must follow change until a reasonably satisfactory solution to the stress has been found. For both Taos and Namhalli, the period of heavy stress has covered approximately one hundred years, perhaps two or three hundred if the very beginnings of the stress are sought. Taos and Namhalli participate, as do most other existing organizations, in a stress situation created by the Industrial Revolution. Because the over-all pattern of changes is highly complex, different organizations have different experiences with it, but all face problems generated by it. Because the period of change will undoubtedly extend beyond the foreseeable future, the problem appears to be one of adapting to external conditions that are changing more rapidly and over a longer period than they ever could have in the past.

CONCLUSION

Stress, particularly when it is complex and of long duration, can be described either in terms of a series of happenings or in terms of organizational response to those happenings. Such a description, however, gives us no over-all picture of the character of the stress; the anthropologist, at the end, is little better off than the rank-and-file membership of the organization. Stress can also be described in terms of those variables that make the real character of the stress easy or difficult to perceive, and that makes the problem posed important enough to be worth solving and easy enough to be solvable. Although these attributes of stresses are partly dependent on an organization's capacity for perceiving and solving problems, an abstract view of stress—one unrelated to any particular organization—gives us a basis for broader comparisons between organizations and for general judgments about the probable effect of stress in a particular case. The concept of stress is useful for understanding both external conditions in general and changing external conditions, for an external condition is merely a stress that has been incorporated into the fabric of problem-solving devices within the organization.

By viewing stress in terms of component variables, we can go far toward resolving controversies concerning both the phenomena of unity in the face of adversity and of disunity in the face of adversity. An organization is likely to present a united front in the face of a stress if the stress occurs as a solvable perceived threat to all members of the organization. Where a stress is not easily perceived, where the problems posed are not easily solved, and where different members of the community receive positive and negative reinforcement from the stress, unity is far less likely. Members of all organizations, faced with unprecedented situations, are bound to try to handle them in a variety of ways. Presumably there is a natural tendency to attempt to solve problems in a unified way before disunity develops, but for an organization to act, it must first recognize a problem worthy of being acted upon, and it must have a structure powerful enough to permit significant activity.

Besides having patterns of strain that made internal conflict probable, Namhalli and Taos were subjected to stresses whose effect on the existing pattern of strains was to make conflict virtually inevitable. First, the stress affecting both communities was only partly visible. A great many things, such as increasing population, were not easily recognized as threatening. Second, there was little order or coherence in the variations in the environment created by the stress. Third, the stress was complex to an unprecedented degree. There was, then, little chance of defining the problem, let alone of solving it. Fourth, the stress involved constraint. Even if the nature of the problem had been clearly understood, it would have been difficult to take appropriate action. Fifth, there was a high degree of selectivity, so that it became difficult to muster consensus concerning the nature of the threat to the community or to obtain acceptance of any particular set of leaders. Probably selectivity is the most important aspect of stress for the development of pervasive factionalism. Where selectivity is low and constraints are applied more impersonally, a tendency toward revitalization movements and messianic cults can be expected. Where there is neither constraint nor selectivity, there may be a tendency toward a more complete solution, such as a closed community or a pattern of avoiding modern influences. A stone struck with a hammer is likely to shatter; a stone struck with a hammer and chisel is likely to crack. But not every stone will shatter or crack predictably. The blows must be struck with a knowledge of the strains and weaknesses characteristic of the particular piece of stone being struck. We say, then, that a stress which is low in visibility, high in randomness, high in complexity, high in constraint, high in selectivity and long in duration is most likely to produce factionalist dispute. This likelihood is maximal if the strain system of the organization is influenced by the stress in such a way as to accentuate existing and potential conflicts.

Stress, particularly (but not exclusively) in the form of urbanization and Westernization, has for years been a favorite *deus ex machina* of the social and behavioral sciences. Hilltown, for example, disintegrated as a result of the building of railroads and the introduction of modern influences generally (Homans, 1950, pp. 357–59). The Tanala changed as they shifted from dry- to wet-rice agriculture (Linton, 1933). Chan Kom rose and fell in response to urban influences (Redfield, 1934, 1950). The Polynesian culture of Moala, it has been asserted, was shaped entirely by adaptation to intercultural relationships and natural influences (Sahlins, 1962, p. 14). Pitt-Rivers, somewhat more cautiously than most authors, expresses the matter as follows (1927, p. 27):

It appears, then, that under certain circumstances when a people fall under the domination of an alien race, which seeks to impose upon it incompatible culture-forms, over-population, or at any rate a rapid increase of population, is likely to occur, partly as a result of breakdown of native customs, which formerly regulated numbers, and partly by inducing a feeling of general discontent or apathy, or by fostering a condition of social disorganization resulting from interference with, or modification of, native cultural elements.

Because the trinity of urbanization, modernization, and Westernization represented the most evident outside influence upon all modern organizations and cultural systems, anthropologists and sociologists have been inclined to regard these things as the source of virtually all cultural change. Study after study has described changing tribes, organizations, or cities without really attempting to describe the outside influences affecting them in any detail. Perhaps most marked in the work of Robert Redfield, following

Park, Burgess, and Tönnies, is the notion of a linear progression from folk to urban. At times it has seemed as if the entire world were moving inexorably toward an ambivalently regarded state of up-to-dateness. This being the case, there was little need to consider the actual nature of the forces causing the movement. All cultural changes appeared to be one in origin, one in nature, and one in effect. Beyond the making of a few minor distinctions, such as that between voluntary and forced acculturation, anthropologists have avoided any close examination of the forces actually influencing the organizations they have studied. Those studies that do pay special attention to the nature of external influences, such as Linton's study of the Tanala (1933), Colson's study of the Makah (1953), and the Kriges' *Realm of a Rain Queen* (1943), tend to deal with such influences in highly specific terms. Rarely are stresses described in general terms; almost never do they form a part of a general theory of culture.

If we are to speak of outside influences as playing a part in the modification of cultural systems, it is essential that there be ways of describing the influences that possess cross-cultural validity—influences, that is, that are objective and generalizable. Without a clear way of describing stresses, there can be no clear comparison of different societies undergoing processes of change. The materials derived from Taos and Namhalli suggest that an objective and general description of stress situations is possible in terms of such dimensions as visibility, randomness, complexity, constraint, selectivity, and duration.

6. Pervasive Factionalism in Namhalli

There is no special instant in Namhalli's history at which the village could be said to have made a transition from normal kinds of conflict to pervasive factionalism. The Ayudha Puja incident, which involved most of the population of the village and led to the abandonment of further attempts at cooperation, may perhaps be regarded as the point at which people in Namhalli finally abandoned the hope that traditional methods of running the community could be made to work.

THE AYUDHA PUJA INCIDENT

The Ayudha Puja is a part of Dasara, a ceremony lasting nine or ten days, which is of great importance throughout Mysore State. During Dasara, the Maharaja of Mysore conducts the most important ceremony himself in the capital city, with pilgrims and tourists from Mysore State and all over the world in attendance. Traditionally, every village and community in the state marked the period of Dasara with celebration and ceremonial, but in 1952 Namhalli had not held a Dasara celebration for ten years. This failure was attributed partly to poor economic conditions, but most particularly to the lack of unanimity within the village.

On September 22, 1952, the important men of Namhalli met on the veranda of the most important village shop and decided to resume the celebration of Dasara with a six-day program of ceremonial. Those present included representatives from all of the important jatis (castes) in the village, among them the village Headman, representing the Jangamas, and representatives of the Shepherd, Smith, Lingayat, Oil Merchant, and Muslim jatis. The only one who made any objection to these plans was the Muslim storekeeper, who said that members of his jati would be prohibited for religious reasons from making any financial contribution to the ceremony. After some discussion, it was decided that the Muslim contribution could be considered an act of charity rather than a contribution to the ceremony. A different jati was to worship Gopalsvami, the village deity, each day: Shepherds would worship on the first day, the low-ranking Madiga on the second, Lingayats and Jangama on the third, Ganiga on the fourth, Blacksmiths and Americans (the ethnographer and his employees) on the fifth, and all the people together on the sixth. Everyone seemed satisfied with the decision, and the meeting broke up amicably.

Five days later, September 27, while the image of Gopalsvami and the temple premises were being made ready for the first day of celebration, the village Headman announced that the Jangama and Lingayat jatis would not participate in the ceremony because they had been assigned the third day of worship rather than the first day, which, as the highest-ranking castes in terms of ceremonial purity, they regarded as their proper privilege. The other castes protested that arrangements had already been made, and that it would be impossible to make any change. It is considered sacrilegious to end a religious ceremony without carrying it to completion, and both the Lingayat-Jangama group and their opponents tried to throw the blame on each other.

In an attempt to reach an agreement, one man representing the Lingayats and Jangamas and another man representing their opponents met to debate the issue. The debate was a draw, and the rest of the jatis decided to go ahead with the ceremony without the Lingayats and Jangamas. They also decided to shorten the length of the ceremony to three days. Thus, on the first day, the Smiths and the Oil Merchants performed the first worship, immediately followed by the Shepherds. Five Lingayat families who were present made offerings after the Shepherds.

The second morning was set aside for the Ayudha Puja, the worship of weapons and implements. Those who owned carts decorated them with flowers and bright-colored powder. After the carts had been worshiped, a procession was to go to the village temple. At this point it was discovered that the Barbers, who have the duty of playing the pipes during processions, were absent and could not be found.

It was then discovered that during the night the Lingayat-Jangama group had borrowed an image of the Lingayat deity, Basavanna, in order to hold a separate ceremony for that deity at the same time as the worship of the carts. The Lingayats had threatened the pipers with violence if they played for the Gopalsvami procession. Finally, after discussion between the two groups, the pipers arrived and the procession started. In the meantime, the Lingayats discovered that the drums they had planned to use in their procession had been locked up in the house of one of the worshipers of Gopalsvami. The Lingayats complained about this to their opponents and were told to ask the village Watchman, who traditionally heads the Madiga jati. The Watchman said that since there had been no notification in advance, it would be impossible for his men to play drums for the Lingayats until the Gopalsvami worship was completed. The Lingayats then threatened to fine the village Watchman. Members of the other group said, "If the Watchman has made a mistake, you also have made many mistakes." After some discussion it was decided once again to appoint representatives of the two groups and have them debate the issue and arrive at a judgment to which all might agree. This time, however, the man who had represented the Lingayats and Jangamas in the first debate was chosen to represent the opponents, and a new man, also a Lingayat, was chosen to represent the Lingayat-Jangama side. The two men debated and announced that everyone should stop quarreling and peacefully carry out the separate functions together, completing the Gopalsvami procession that day and the Basavanna procession the next morning.

When the decision was announced, the Lingayat-Jangama group announced that they must start their procession immediately because they had promised to return the image of Basavanna by noon of the next day. Their opponents countered with protests that their procession would have to continue as scheduled because they could not return the deity to the temple without finishing the procession. It was suggested that the Lingayats place the image of Basavanna in front of the Gopalsvami temple, referred to as the Government temple, and that everyone worship it there. But the Lingayats reiterated their intention of holding their procession immediately, and the other group replied that it would be impossible to celebrate a procession in honor of Basavanna on a day set aside for the worship of implements. While this prolonged argument was going on, most of the village cattle were standing in the sun, along with the other participants in the procession. Finally, an old man shouted angrily that his cattle were thirsty.

Abandoning the debate, the Gopalsvami worshipers resumed their procession and the Lingayats and Jangamas withdrew. The next step in the procession had to do with the worship of the stones marking the traditional gateway of the village. It was a ritual that had to be performed by a member of the Jangama jati, but the man who was usually entitled to perform the ritual refused to do so. Finally, another Jangama agreed to take his place. Parenthetically, it may be noted that in the course of the dispute no single jati was successful in imposing a boycott on either the Lingayat-Jangama group or their opponents, except the Madiga jati, which not only refused to drum for the Lingayats but was prepared to beat with sticks any drummers brought in from outside.

A large part of the village population participated in the Gopalsvami procession, and an almost equally large number appeared in the evening for the worship of Basavanna. At the Basavanna ceremony, a pancayat meeting was held for the purpose of passing judgment on the Jangama who had violated the Lingayat boycott of the Gopalsvami procession. After considerable argument it was decided to forget the incident and to carry out the procession of Basavanna the next morning, Monday, September 29, without any further quarreling.

The procession went off without incident, partly, perhaps, because the image of Basavanna, instead of being taken to every house in the village, was taken only to the houses of Jangamas and Lingayats. At the Gopalsvami temple, preparations were made for the second phase of the Ayudha Puja. As a variation on the previous day's arrangement, the image of Gopalsvami was placed on a cart, both the deity and the cart being profusely decorated with flowers. Just as the procession was to begin, at two o'clock in the afternoon, heavy rain clouds appeared, ending the drought that had nearly ruined all the unirrigated crops raised by the villagers. The procession was postponed until evening, and to while away the time, several members of the Gopalsvami group sent out for liquor, which they consumed in quantity. When the rain stopped, the cart with Gopalsvami again got under way. As it left the temple, the procession passed under a tamarind tree owned by one of the Jangamas, but the image of the deity on the cart was too high to pass freely. Some insisted that the tree be cut; others took ropes and ladders and attempted to raise the branches so that the image could pass under them. When they saw what was happening, the village Headman and other members of the Jangama-Lingayat group rushed out, shouting that Gopalsvami should be removed from the cart and the tree left undisturbed. In the excitement, the Headman laid hands on one of the Gopalsvami group. Thereupon another Gopalsvami man who happened to live close by rushed into his house and got a large sword. His friends quickly subdued him, and at last succeeded in raising the branch and taking Gopalsvami under the tree.

The next stage in the procession was a ceremony in honor of the implements, held on top of a hill outside the village. The ceremony represented the recovery of their weapons by the five Pandava brothers after their long exile, and the beginning of the great war in which, according to the *Mahabharata*, the noble Kshatriya line was destroyed. The ceremony was duly performed, and the procession returned to the village. After some argument, it was decided to return to the temple by the same route as before. Trouble was expected at the tamarind tree, but the Lingayat group had left. After passing the tree, "the procession was stopped on account of rain and making those drunkards peaceful was a great job," as an educated member of the group remarked. The image of the deity was left outside the temple.

During the night members of the Gopalsvami group assembled and discussed ways of settling the conflict. It was decided to form a pancayat or committee of neutrals who would decide upon the means of bringing peace to the village. The pancayat, which consisted mainly of Lingayats including their two representatives at the earlier debates, met in front of the schoolhouse. The decision was that the Gopalsvami procession should be completed first and then the branch of the tree cut. The Gopalsvami group rejected the decision—the tree branch must be cut before the procession, not after. The Lingayats refused to contemplate the suggestion that they cut off a branch of a fruit-bearing tree, which they considered a sacrilege.

The following morning, September 30, the village Headman went to the nearby town to file a complaint against the village Watchman for failing to provide drummers for the Basavanna ceremony. He also planned to bring a police constable to prevent completion of the Gopalsvami ceremony. Members of the opposition also went to the town, carrying a petition denouncing the Headman and prepared to pay a fifty-rupee bribe. This marked the first time that any members of the village had attempted to secure police assistance in order to settle an internal dispute. The next day, October 1, the police entered the village and took representatives of both groups to the police station. Later in the afternoon, the police returned with the representatives and supervised while the village Watchman cut off the offending branch.

There was little violence in the Ayudha Puja incident, and no one was injured. Upon previous occasions intravillage conflicts had been considerably more violent. Much more important was the interpretation given to the conflict within the village. The appeal to the police, far from settling the conflict, provided the Lingayat group with fresh grounds for criticism of their opponents. Furthermore, whereas all previous large-scale conflicts within the village had been resolved in one way or another, the Ayudha Puja incident remained unresolved, and the annual ceremonies upon which the traditional system rested went unperformed. To be sure, cooperative undertakings within the village had been progressively declining since 1941, but the Ayudha Puja conflict brought all types of village-wide cooperation to a halt. The uniqueness of the Ayudha Puja incident rests upon the involvement of most of the village population in the dispute, the failure of all attempts at arbitration, and finally the appeal to outside authority, which also proved unable to resolve the dispute.

THE MEMBERSHIP OF THE DISPUTING GROUPS

One way of explaining the events connected with the Ayudha Puja incident is to consider the social origins of the members of the two opposing sides, and the relevance of these two groupings to the social structure of the village as expressed through other groupings. The key figure in the dispute was the village Headman, a Jangama. It was he who first refused to participate in the Ayudha Puja, and it was he who arranged for the performance of the Basavanna Puja. With the village Headman were associated a number of related families belonging to the Jangama or Lingayat Priest jati. Out of the sixty persons in this jati, only one family supported the opposition. The Headman's success in mobilizing members of his own jati can be attributed to his kinship bonds with members of his jati and to the ideological basis that he attributed to the dispute. The Headman claimed that he and his jati were entitled to ceremonial and political benefits by virtue of the traditional standing of the jati. On several occasions during the dispute, the Headman went so far as to claim suzerainty of the village; he refused to go to the town to discuss matters with the police unless the Sub-Inspector agreed to send an airplane to transport him there. To be sure, the Headman and his jati had suffered a decline in ceremonial and political status over the years, but the Headman's claim that he was merely seeking a return to the old and proper way of doing things was hardly justified by the facts. For one thing, the traditional organization of the village had been based on the consent of the governed, and the Headman clearly envisioned a reimposition of his authority supported by the police power of government. The Headman appealed to traditional values and presented himself as a conservative, but he was in fact a radical seeking powers and privileges that had never belonged to his ancestors.

The next largest group of the Headman's supporters was drawn from the Lingayat Farmer jati (96 members). In the main, these consisted of the followers and sycophants of a single wealthy man (the man chosen by the Lingayats for the second debate), representing roughly one-third of the membership of the Lingayats. In addition, this man commanded the support of several families of Weavers and Shepherds who were aligned with him through economic ties or through illegitimate descent from himself or one of his three brothers. He had been opposed for years in his own jati by another man, who brought approximately one-third of the Lingayats onto the other side in the Ayudha Puja controversy. The remaining third of the Lingayat jati attempted to maintain neutrality in the dispute, either by staying home or by attending the ceremonials held by both sides. One influential Lingayat, who represented his jati in the first debate, shifted to the opposition, along with his brother, but ultimately shifted back again when some members of the opposition attempted to cheat the brother out of his lands. In other words, the Lingayats, though they would have stood to gain a good deal from having the village run by Lingayat Priests, were not swayed by the Headman's arguments, and proceeded to divide themselves between both parties in pursuit of their own interests. A similar division occurred in the Oil Merchant jati, which consisted of two families run by brothers who were feuding. The elder brother sided with the Lingayats after it became apparent that the younger brother was identified with the opposition.

The Pancala jati, which maintained a traditional hostility toward the Jangama jati, and the Muslims, who had the least to gain from the emergence of a Hindu theocracy run by the Headman, were both unanimously identified with the opposition. Each of these jatis contained about fifty persons, and kinship probably played a major role in their alignment with the opposition, since the Pancala were all descendants of the same grandfather, and the Muslims were related by lineage and marital ties. Among the Ganigas and the Lingayats, the alternative affiliation with the two sides was also decided on the basis of kinship, in this case on the basis of antagonism between close relatives.

The Shepherd jati, which contained 126 members, was also mainly affiliated with the opposition, though perhaps one-fifth sided with the Lingayats, again mainly for family reasons. The 61-member Weaver jati and the 107-member Madiga jati, both of which were poor, seemed to belong to whichever side had the most power over them as individuals at any given moment. Exceptions to this rule were the Headman of the Madiga jati, who sided publicly with the opposition, and two wealthy families of the Weaver jati, who sided publicly with the Lingayats. Of the numerically unimportant jatis, the Hunters sided with the opposition and the remainder tried to stay aloof. The Washermen and the Barbers, who had important ceremonial roles and could not remain aloof, were compelled to side with the opposition. Brahmins, none of whom were permanent residents, also sided with the opposition.

It would be possible to define the membership of the Lingayat-Jangama side as consisting of tradition-oriented people, or simply of the Lingayat-Jangama jatis, and to define the opposition as consisting of progressive, non-Lingayat jatis. It appears more likely, however, that membership in one faction or another was based not upon traditional cleavages within the village, but rather upon pre-existing relationships of hostility, which people sought to work out by joining the factions that contained the smallest proportion of their enemies, or their less important enemies. In the Lingayat jati, the wealthy man with one-third of the jati on his side, was hostile to the village Headman, but he was even more hostile to the leaders of the Pancala jati. The other leading Lingayat member, although inclined by personality toward neutrality, switched to the opposition in order to express his hostility toward his Lingayat enemy. The Oil Merchant who sided with the Lingayats did so solely because his hated brother was a leading member of the opposition. Probably the ideological implications of the dispute were the purest window dressing. What was really involved was an opportunistic desire to get back at one's enemies by joining an appropriate faction. No one really cared whether Gopalsvami traveled in a cart or in a palanquin, and no one considered it a sacrilege to cut a branch from a fruit-bearing tree. The village Headman no doubt believed that the government, with its talk about village self-government and the restoration of the good old ways, would support his position, but it is unlikely that anyone else really hoped for the establishment of a Hindu theocracy run by the Headman. Nor was the Lingayat-Jangama decision to provoke a quarrel with the numerically and economically superior Gopalsvami group really so irrational as it may seem, for had they received the government support they expected (since their leader was a government official), they would have scored an easy victory. As a result of his defeat, the village Headman lost both his official position and his position as a village leader. The Lingayats who had opposed him in the quarrel refused to have anything more to do with him, and so did several of his relatives whose small businesses had suffered as a result of the dispute. In defeat, then, the Lingayat-Jangama alignment collapsed, and some of the subgroups that had been part of it also ceased to exist in any organized fashion. In victory, the opposition secured the appointment of a member of the Shepherd jati as village Headman; but quarrels between the new Headman and other members of his side soon developed, and this faction collapsed in its turn.

Both sides of the controversy had begun to form in the spring of 1952, when the village Headman announced that he would hold a firewalking ceremony. It is the tradition in Namhalli for all village ceremonials to be attended by every member of the village, or at least by persons representing each house or each jati. The firewalking ceremony, however, by a separate tradition, was supposed to be restricted to Lingayats, although the tradition had in fact been ignored in the vicinity for a considerable period of time. Over the protest of the religious specialist whom he had hired to conduct the ceremony, the Headman decided that participation in the firewalking would be limited to Jangamas and Lingayats, the implication being that members of other jatis were too sinful and polluted to attempt firewalking and would burn their feet.

Previously the major dispute in the village had been between the Headman and the rich Lingayat whose supporters later formed the core of the Lingayat-Jangama alliance. This man had brought suit against the Headman, claiming that the Headman had built his house on public lands. Shortly after the firewalking ceremony, in which the rich Lingayat had participated, he dropped his case against the Headman, preparing the ground for the alliance. His chief enemy in the Lingayat jati had taken an enthusiastic part in the firewalking, though, as we have seen, he eventually ended up in the opposition. At the firewalking, a number of non-Lingayats organized a competitive procession in honor of Gopalsvami, but on this occasion there were no incidents beyond some shouted comments when the procession passed the scene of the firewalking. This expressed opposition was an opposition between Lingayats and non-Lingayats, but the fragile unity of the Lingayats had been destroyed a few months later, by the time of the Ayudha Puja.

Both sides existed during a single summer, and during that summer they both increased their membership until there were virtually no neutrals left in the community. Even during this summer, however, there were several shifts in membership, the most spectacular by the Lingayat who represented his jati in the first debate over the Ayudha Puja affair, switched to the opposition, and later switched back when he discovered that some opposition members were cheating his brother. Another notable defector was the Jangama who participated in a Gopalsvami ceremonial. In addition, several Lingayat families shifted from a position on the fringes of the Lingayat-Jangama group to wholehearted participation in the opposition, and some families of Shepherds and Weavers shifted from the opposition to the Lingayat-Jangama side.

These temporary alignments were not based upon firmly established cleavages within the community; rather, they were alliances for the moment, often among persons who were accustomed to being at odds with one another. Neither group possessed any particularly strong ideological basis, although they both made an effort to take firm, if not necessarily consistent, ideological positions.

THE BACKGROUND OF THE AYUDHA PUJA INCIDENT

As we have noted, the summer of 1952 was one of severe drought. Nothing resembling famine conditions threatened, but the poor quality of the harvest from the unirrigated lands of the village was a severe economic blow. There was also anxiety lest the water stored in the irrigation reservoir be diverted from the village rice fields to those of a wealthy landlord on the other side of the valley. It was believed that even if the government awarded the water to Namhalli, the landlord would blow up a part of the dam so that the water would flow out on his side of the valley. For some twelve years previous, Namhalli had enjoyed unprecedented prosperity. World War II had introduced Namhalli to a new world of bus travel, motion pictures, and other costly urban amusements and gimcracks. The years immediately following the war represented some decline in the prosperity of the village, but crops and grain prices remained high. But the bad year of 1952 brought home to even the least informed members of the village the fact that opportunities for outside employment were shrinking, and that the traditional agricultural economy of the village could not possibly support the rising population, half of which was under twelve years of age.

But though the times were troublesome, the village made no attempt to propose fresh solutions to the problems confronting it. On the contrary, old patterns of conflict merely became intensified, to the point where almost every meaningful interpersonal relationship became affected. In some cases, traditional devices for resolving conflict were sufficient to deal with the problem. In other cases, the conflicts could not be resolved, and the time was ripe for the establishment of those relationships of permanent hostility which, as we have seen, played a key role in the development of the Ayudha Puja incident. Some of these took a violent form.

Conflict across generations

On September 21, 1952, a week before the Ayudha Puja incident, a young man took a gold sovereign from the joint family savings of his father and his father's brother and used it to buy jewelry. Previously his parents had refused to buy him a wrist-watch or gold rings on the grounds that "times were bad." On April 19, 1953, the same young man took one hundred rupees from the family account and went off to the city, where he spent the money on clothes and entertainment. Six days later he sold his schoolbooks and used the money to buy film magazines. Because of this behavior, the boy's father was forced to break with his brother and set up a separate household. The boy's father also made hasty arrangements to marry his son to a woman residing in another village. The son said, "My father-in-law has many lands, a radio, and twenty-five cattle. Because he is so rich, I don't care whether my family supports me or not. Though my parents send me out of their house, I can go to my father-in-law's house and live safely."

In another family, where there were five sons, the father refused his sons' requests to buy them new clothing, nor would he give them money for a theatrical performance being organized by the young men of the village. Then one of the sons stole a silver leg chain from his sister-in-law and sold it in order to get enough money to pay for a trip to visit relatives in a distant town. Finally, in April 1953, the five brothers together took some money and bought clothing for themselves. When the father learned what they had done, he left the house. "So he is not talking with us, he is not coming to the house, but we are supplying food near the garden. We asked him to buy us some tailored clothing. He said I won't do it, so we ourselves purchased some." In both of these cases, the sons wanted to dress and behave in the fashion of the urban middle or lower middle class. In both cases the parents objected, but were unable to enforce their authority. In neither case could the disputes be arbitrated. The result was a permanent breakdown in familial relationships.

On July 11, 1952, a son locked his father out of the house and threatened to kill him. The father and his sons divided their property a few months later, but the father would not allow his children to farm the land that they had been awarded when the family separated, and he refused to pay land taxes on it. On July 30, 1952, a father refused to give money to his grown son, and the son threatened to cut his father into three pieces. In another family an adult son committed suicide because his father and elder brother were making him work hard, but not giving him adequate food or arranging his marriage. A similar case of mistreatment involved an orphaned brother and sister who were being mistreated by an uncle. More minor incidents recorded during the period June 1952 to August 1953 involved several cases where the son refused to accept the marital arrangements proposed by his parents, and several cases where a father or a son refused to attend a wedding or a funeral that the other had arranged. In addition there were many complaints of the following sort: "The son told me that his father had no sense. His father was accustomed to giving away the food that is brought to him, to poor people. The son is used to eating lunch after working in the fields. The father is used to starving without food until dinner time."

Although such cross-generational differences occur in many societies, the authority structure of Namhalli seemed particularly ill-equipped to deal with them. In the face of the most flagrant violations of the rules governing appropriate behavior, the community was mute. People were scandalized, but no action was taken except to prevent severe physical injury.

Four recorded cases of family division, believed in Namhalli to originate in quarrels among the womenfolk, were actually the result of cross-generational conflicts. Two cases have already been mentioned. In another case, a man's mother and his wife insisted that he buy jewels for the wife. In this case, the dispute was settled when a pancayat decided that the young people should live separately from the parents. Another man announced that he did not like his brothers or his parents because they spent his earnings on eating and drinking instead of on arrangements for his marriage. Again, the result was a division of the family.

Conflict between brothers

Conflict between brothers appears to occur after the parents have died, either at the time of family division or afterward when the younger brothers realize that the elder brother has cheated them. In addition to four or five permanently established conflicts between brothers such as the case of the two oil merchants described earlier, there were in this period of observation two fresh outbursts of hostility between brothers who had formerly been friendly. In one case, two brothers quarreled over ownership of a tamarind tree and over the younger's refusal to lend the elder money. The elder beat the younger unconscious with a stick. Neighbors carried the younger brother to town, where they intended to report the assault to the police; but he revived on the way and persuaded them not to, so the conflict remained unresolved. In an undivided family, the eldest brother refused to work on the grounds that he was head of the family, and the next-eldest also refused to work on the grounds that the eldest was not working. This dispute was resolved, but the second brother announced that he would leave the family at the first available opportunity. The relationship between brothers in Namhalli continues to be one of the most stable relationships in the village, and it is also the most sacred relationship, perhaps as important as that between parents and children. It should be said that although conflict between generations and between siblings does not account for any very large proportion of the conflict in the village, it is the most shocking kind of conflict and the most contrary to traditional values.

Husband-wife conflict

Between the end of June 1952 and the end of April 1953, some sixteen families were involved in disputes between husband and wife. Five of these conflicts led to divorce, three to separation, one to the departure of a family from the village, and four to reconciliation (three were too complicated to classify). This list includes only major public conflicts in which a number of people became involved. Most of the recorded conflicts involved adultery on the part of the wife, and many involved a series of incidents stretching over several months. The most sensational of these involved three brothers, the youngest of whom apparently suffered from some sort of physiological or psychological defect. His elder brothers arranged two marriages for him, at his expense, and then attempted to sleep with his wives. In 1952, the youngest brother, having been twice divorced, took a third wife, but after three months of quarreling he accused her of trying to poison him. It appeared that the accusation was really a subterfuge designed to obtain a favorable disposition of the jewelry and property that had been given to the wife by the husband's family at the time of the marriage. After a good deal of discussion and open conflict between Namhalli and the wife's village, a divorce was arranged. The following spring the youngest brother acquired a fourth wife, who promptly jumped in a well and nearly drowned. In the subsequent discussion, the three brothers refused to permit the wife to return to her family. After a month of threats and exhortations, her parents succeeded in extricating her from her predicament, and she walked out of the village carrying a small black suitcase and wearing a stubborn expression.

In the more usual divorce case, the husband hears that his wife is unfaithful, gives her a thorough drubbing, and then waits to see if she behaves. Later, on the strength of further rumors or discoveries, he beats her again and she leaves the house or is thrown out. Occasionally, the wife remains in the village, evidently hoping for forgiveness, until her relatives come and take her away; but in other cases she leaves at once for her parents' house, taking only her very young children. If reconciliation occurs, it is generally through the intervention of interested neighbors. In one case, the husband became lonely for his children and asked his wife to return. Rarely are there sharply drawn lines to mark the various stages of quarreling, separation, divorce, and reconciliation. It may be years, perhaps not until remarriage is contemplated, before a divorce will be formalized by a pancayat decision, followed by the return of jewels or property acquired by the husband or wife as part of the marriage agreement. If the dispute is a particularly bitter one, remarriage may occur without benefit of any formal divorce negotiations. Although both adultery and formal divorce were probably rather frequent in traditional times, few modern instances of husband-wife conflict are settled by formal arbitration. The basic rule governing the arbitration is that if the divorce is a result of the husband's ill treatment of the wife, the wife can keep the wedding jewelry; if the divorce is the wife's fault, she cannot. None of the divorces occurring during 1952–53 was settled in this way. Ordinarily either the husband snatched away the wife's jewelry or the wife fled to her native village with it. Whatever the further discussion or arbitration, the one who had the jewelry kept it. Arbitration was effective only in those cases where the husband and wife seemed to desire reconciliation or where attempts at rape were involved. Three cases of attempted rape occurred, but only one led to a conflict between a wife and husband. In two of the cases, the person who attempted rape was expelled from the village after being fined or beaten.

Borrowers and lenders

Between April 1952 and June 1953, seventeen cases of conflict between borrowers and lenders were recorded in the field notes. Three of these cases were resolved, and two were partly resolved. In the remaining cases, the borrower refused to repay the loan. Often the behavior of the borrower amounted to outright theft. For example, one borrower seized a promissory note from his creditor's hand and refused to repay it. In two cases, the borrower fled from the village. In other cases, where the loans and other obligations involved relatively small amounts, the borrower simply refused to repay the money. In a few cases, the creditor recovered the amount owed him by force. Many of these cases led to the expression of enmity, the loser threatening revenge or the disputants coming to blows. Often the wrongdoer was scolded by his relatives and ended up quarreling with them as well. One man beat his wife for paying the money due on a bicycle he had rented; a father threatened to desert his family unless his son reformed; and so on. Persons who attempted to settle unresolved disputes were likely to be drawn into the conflict on one side or another. The conflict tended to spread in ever-widening circles limited only by the energy of the participants and the distraction created by fresh conflicts.

Minor thefts of clothing, umbrellas, grain, agricultural equip-

ment, hay, and manure were not recorded systematically. In most
cases the thief was known, but few owners succeeded in recovering
their property. Only chronic thieves and servants were likely to be
punished. A man who was observed repeatedly stealing hay was
caught and fined. Servants hired on a yearly basis to assist in agricultural operations succeeded on several occasions in absconding
with cattle or property. When they were caught they were beaten.
In landlord-tenant relationships, which usually involved persons of
more or less equal status or local people and absentee landowners,
the landowners without exception were dissatisfied because their
tenants either failed to manure the fields properly or failed to report their harvest accurately, giving the landlord far less than his
usual 50 per cent. The landlord's only recourse was to change tenants, but no one was ever satisfied with the new tenants. If the
landlord abandons all hope and leaves his fields uncultivated, disputes are likely to develop over who should farm the field illicitly.

Part of the background of conflict within the village consists of
long-standing disputes over the ownership of particular parcels of
land. These disputes, many of them reaching back into the 1920's
and 1930's, invariably lead to permanent enmity. A good example
is the dispute between the two Lingayats that caused them to take
opposite sides in the Ayudha Puja incident. Jati membership was
usually not an issue in disputes. Occasionally a Shepherd was
teased about sheepshearing, and sometimes Jangamas became
abusive in defense of their jati purity, but in no case could these
incidents be described as tense or leading to enmity. Tempers occasionally flared during the almost daily volleyball games played
by the young men of the village, but never to any serious extent.

EFFECTS OF CONFLICT

The mere fact of frequent conflict is not sufficient to indicate
either a process of change in social relationships or the emergence
of pervasive factionalism. The unique aspect of conflict in Namhalli is its impact upon cooperation within the community. Conflict, no matter how frequent, that occurs in noncritical relationships, or that is consistently resolved or brought to an end, is very

different from conflict that occurs in critical relationships and is not resolved. Conflict in Namhalli occurs in many critical relationships: between brothers, between parents and children, between husbands and wives, between borrowers and lenders, between masters and servants. Conflicts in all these relationships often remain unresolved, and the effect of these unresolved conflicts upon the village is all too clear. Members of the community distrust one another, and there has been a great decline in the various cooperative activities upon which the village depends in order to accomplish its goals.

The citizens of Namhalli, in 1952–53, expressed contempt for fellow members of the community in general and were prepared to give details about the sinful and criminal activities of almost everyone. The following remarks are typical:

Here is what you should tell foreigners. India is full of deceit. Any man who becomes wealthy through his own labors will not be tolerated by others; they will ruin him one way or another.

The people here are immoral and too eager to earn money by hook or by crook.

Money is such that if any trustworthy person gets money he will change and spend the money on himself or his own people.

You can add this reason also, especially for this village. There is no unity in this village, and no one person or set of persons controlling the village, and every houseowner in this village considers himself a great man. That's why the village is in this condition.

In more or less nondirective life-history interviews, many informants spent most of their time reciting the life histories, not of themselves, but of their neighbors. One of the leading men of the village, a Blacksmith, became wealthy, it was said, by stealing metal telephone poles from the government. Another village leader became wealthy by poisoning his wife's mother, who was a prostitute, and stealing her jewelry. A Weaver "deceived not only me but almost all the villagers in the sale of farmlands." Even innocent questions about the weather drew replies like the following: "We will not get rain when there is a lot of sin accumulated. People are not recognizing the difference between wife and sister. Sometimes they do worse than that. For example, P——, a Weaver, who had his own daughter as his mistress, is still living. So no rain will come." Although the important men of Namhalli invariably described themselves as unfailingly moral and deeply committed to the welfare of their fellow citizens, their fellow citizens accused all but one or two grandfathers of the most atrocious crimes. Where it might be expected that most communities would be composed mainly of good men with a few bad men on the fringes, people in Namhalli appeared to think of their community as being composed largely of bad people, with a few good people thrown in simply to provide targets for the machinations of the bad people.

For all the widespread distrust, most of the people in the village seem to have been taken in repeatedly. For example, people went on lending money informally without a signed promissory note despite the high odds against being repaid. It was as if some need to trust others led people time and again into unwise transactions. It appears that the average person is torn between a fantasy world in which the traditional familistic interdependence of the village still persists, and a reality in which almost every man feels that he must put his own interests first.

The series of disputes between July 1952 and August 1953, which included the Ayudha Puja incident, brought cooperative activities, at least those carried out on a village-wide basis, to a standstill. With only a few exceptions, this condition persisted until 1958. The most common cause of temporary unity was the belief that thieves might be at work in the casuarina plantations to the west of the village. Once in 1953 and twice in 1954, most of the male population of the village, alarmed by strange noises or rumors, rushed to the road near the plantation armed with sticks and other weapons. Collaborative activity also occurred when heinous crimes such as rape or poisoning were suspected. These were all outside threats of a shocking character that could be dealt with immediately, violently, and safely. But other village-wide functions—the control of minor thievery, the maintenance of ditches and drains, the allocation of irrigation water, the leveling of cart roads, and goverment-subsidized village improvements—were not carried out. Fruit trees in village fields were cut up for firewood. Soon after the Ayudha Puja incident, members of the opposition side gave a theatrical performance that was attended by people from the Lingayat-Jangama side; but the purpose of the performance—to collect money for a reading room—was defeated when the organizers used the funds for their own purposes.

In 1956, the first chit fund was organized in the village by members of the opposition side. The chit fund (contributed capital lent out by an auction system) was successful and included several persons of the Lingayat-Jangama side. Sometime in 1956 or 1957, the village temple (Gopalsvami) was robbed of some images of the deity and certain brass and copper vessels. The thieves were believed to be from the village, but they were not caught. In 1957, a group of young men and boys collected funds for a ceremony that was attended by the entire community. Again, in 1958, the Pancala received agreement from all members of the community when they requested permission to bring the image of Gopalsvami from a neighboring village for a procession. In 1959, a chit fund was set up for the purpose of holding ceremonies honoring the deity Rama.

Although the loss of the village deity, as well as a tendency for minor theft and graft to continue at a fairly high level, made it impossible by January 1960 to resume the pattern of traditional ceremonial and village-wide cooperation, there had been a virtual cessation of hostilities during the period 1953–60. In 1959, the new Headman cheated the villagers out of funds designed to be used to rebuild the temple of the village deity. Attempts to punish him were discouraged and finally abandoned. This suggests a far more relaxed attitude toward minor dishonesty; it also suggests that the old ethic of handling village disputes within the village had regained its former strength.

In 1953, when a man committed suicide by jumping into the village drinking-water well, there was no attempts to clean it out. In 1960, when thieves threw portions of a slaughtered goat into the well used by the lower castes in the village, it was promptly cleaned out. Again, in 1960, the road leading from the bus stop to the village was beautifully maintained and the road through the village had stone curbs. Without question, there had been a decline in the frequency of conflict within the community and a corresponding increase in the effectiveness of cooperative activities.

This change appears to have developed as a result of radical changes in the nature of the stresses affecting the community. Specifically, the expansion of nearby factories had created a situation uniquely advantageous to Namhalli and neighboring villages. First, because the factories provided bus service for their laborers, it was possible for people to live in Namhalli and commute to the factory. Second, because the factories and other associated urban developments expanded the population of the city of Bangalore, the market for agricultural produce of a kind that was free from price control was expanded. In this case, urban influence meant a reinforcement of familial bonds, particularly in a situation in which one brother worked at a factory for cash wages and the other brother raised food on the family plot. The chit fund made it possible for the entire village to accumulate capital more rapidly, and this in turn resulted in improvements necessary for branching out into such lucrative enterprises as vegetable and fruit production. Between 1952 and 1960, Namhalli's population *decreased* from 603 persons living in 106 households to 542 persons living in 113 households. This does not necessarily mean that the family as an economic unit or the village as an economic unit had become smaller. Easy economic conditions in 1960 permitted more families to live separately and enabled more persons to live outside the village, but it also meant that those who remained to farm had the responsibility of caring for the fields, cattle, and timber groves of those who had left. In a sense, interaction between persons in or of the village have become less frequent and more profitable. Family unity in 1960 could be expressed more in terms of mutual profit and less in terms of obligation. In the same way, village unity, being no longer a condition of survival, had ceased to be expected. The chit fund, which was managed by relatively few people, could be used for such purposes as repairing temples or providing bus trips for the schoolchildren, without involving the total population of the village.

7. Pervasive Factionalism in Taos

In 1907 a group of young men from Taos visited a Kiowa group in Oklahoma. There they were initiated into the mysteries of peyote and its associated ritual, songs, tales, and other symbols. Upon their return to Taos they continued to take the drug, but, according to the brief accounts of its history in the pueblo by Parsons (1936, 1939) and Lasswell (1935), it stirred up little opposition. Apparently some proselytizing went on, but on a modest scale. We are informed only that a negative reaction was expressed by one man, a shaman from a prominent family, who felt that the new uses of peyote interfered with the effectiveness of his own curing practices.

It was not until the peyote-centered activities of this small group of practitioners came to be more formalized that the shaman could secure a following among the councilors and organize a concerted opposition. The basis of his support lay in the fact that peyote ritual took time away from traditional ceremonial and, it was argued, weakened the power of collective religious activity. Furthermore, it interfered with the rules of the "quiet period" during the winter season. Once the authorities and custodians of traditional collective ritual had been co-opted into one side of the controversy, they began to use other, less straightforward, arguments. It was not good for the gods, it would interfere with rainmaking, and so on.

The meetings of the peyote cult were held on Saturday nights, and the young men would be unconscious most of the following day. Families customarily went on picnics on Sundays, so that tensions within the family and between in-laws flared into open conflict over the neglect of these and other collective rituals by the "boys." The shaman and his family, and subsequently other politico-religious leaders, exploited these emerging strains, and the controversy blossomed into a disturbing crisis. The conflict lasted for a generation or more. The dates and details of the incidents that punctuated this period are only sketchily known, since except for one event no outside observer was on hand to record specifically what happened or to interview disputants during or immediately after the fact.

About two years after peyote eating and associated practices had been introduced, the Town Crier announced preparations for a major autumn solstice ceremonial held in conjunction with the saint's day festival. Participants were named, and kiva responsibilities designated. Among those who were named as participants were several members of the peyote cult, but they showed their irresponsibility and indifference to the affair by failing to appear at all practice sessions, particularly when they interfered with peyote ceremonies, and by performing badly when they did attend. Not only were they scolded for their behavior, but it was brought angrily to the attention of their fathers and of the heads of other kivas. One father took issue with the accusers, siding with his son. Another father was greatly upset by his son's conduct and argued heatedly with him, but to no avail. In all, about nine or ten young men were involved in family conflicts. Fathers-in-law, who were at the same time among the accusers, added fuel to the fire by challenging those fathers who sided with their sons. In due course the pueblo ceremonial was held, but it was said to have been badly performed by many participants and therefore an affront to the gods. Appeal to traditional controls, family heads, and secular-priest authorities was only partly effective. The ineffectiveness of traditional control figures reflected a weakening of this mechanism for the settling of disputes.

The quarrels arising out of the peyote dispute were many and grew in bitterness. Father was pitted against son, family against family, in-laws against in-laws, and certain members of one ceremonial society against those of another. Through all this, the original small group of peyote users did not capitulate, despite punitive actions, arrests, and even corporal punishment. On one occasion the sheriff and the Council, on the order of the Cacique, raided a session of the peyote cult and arrested all who were present. After a period of detention in the jail, the peyote users were tried individually, at which time each defendant was asked whether he would leave the cult and submit to the Council's authority. The two ranking secular officers of the pueblo, the governor and lieutenant-governor, were among those prosecuted. The former resigned and the latter was removed from office. The rest suffered confiscation of their lands.

At the time of the raid, the Cacique and the Council had also supplied neighboring pueblos with names and descriptions of the arrested men. Shortly afterward, San Juan refused hospitality to two men, not peyote users, who happened to be traveling south; erring on the safe side, citizens of San Juan considered all Taos persons dangerous. On another occasion members of the peyote cult took their case to the Pueblo Agency in Albuquerque, which refused to interfere in the dispute. By extending the base of power outside the pueblo and by inviting the exercise of external sanctions, both sides were in effect resorting to alien sources for conflict resolution, an admission of inability to settle disputes in terms of locally developed techniques.

The matter did not end here. Peyote adherents once more, and this time successfully, took their case outside the pueblo to the courts, where they argued in terms of religious freedom, a concept completely foreign to pueblo standards. Today the issue is dead, although smoldering resentment by members of the hierarchy has not entirely disappeared. Membership in the cult is not large, amounting to no more than sixty or seventy persons out of a population of more than 1,200. Since all members are male, however, the actual percentage of the whole must be doubled. Full commitment to both ceremonial and secular collaborative activities has never been achieved since the termination of this conflict. "The net effect of the Peyote innovation," Fenton observed (1957, p. 327), "was to break up family solidarity. Informal sanctions within

families drove some individuals to renounce peyote, but schisms
and tensions remain."

Although the peyote controversy might be said to have ended,
in the late 1940's another outbreak of disputes arose upon the
return of veterans following World War II. A series of episodes
occurred, largely initiated by the veterans, which culminated in a
confrontation in the pueblo that ended just short of open fighting
between a faction dominated by old men in the Council and another headed by the younger men. In what follows we shall attempt to describe the nature of these events in the approximate
order of their occurrence. The data in this section were collected
partly by Bernard J. Siegel and partly by Fenton (1957) during a
brief but intensive series of interviews with members of the pueblo
hierarchy.

During the years 1946 and 1947 a number of the veterans wanted
to wear their military uniforms to visit the graves of fallen com-
rades whose bodies had been removed to the pueblo for burial.
On another occasion a group of friends asked the Council for permission to hold a dance at the school (actually government property), with phonograph music. Two veterans were planning to set
up businesses for which they petitioned that they be allowed to
bring in electricity. In all these issues they were thwarted by
negative action taken by the dominant element within the Council.
On each occasion the petitioners sought to ally with them fathers,
fathers-in-law, respected elders of the kiva societies, or one of the
secular officials. They usually succeeded in doing so, but they
never succeeded in swinging the final vote in their favor. Membership in these groups changed with the issue. The grave-visiting
petition involved nearly all of the pueblo's hundred-odd war veterans, and more than half of their fathers strongly supported them.
Two members of the Council, in opposition to the dominant kiva
chief, also joined in advocating consent. However, certain of the
younger men who were not war veterans supported the Council
majority. Fewer persons were involved in the dance petition, and

the alignment of contending parties was rather different. In neither of these cases did the argument come to a complete impasse. It became necessary, however, to resort to the rarely invoked mechanism of absenteeism from crucial Council meetings by dissenting elders in order to maintain the fiction of unanimity of action (a necessary requirement for the resolution of any conflict). There has been a striking rise in the use of this mechanism since the war.

Many lesser conflicts between individual members of the pueblo that to some extent affect the community as a whole have also arisen. One of these is worth mentioning at some length, since it was carefully observed and discussed during a fieldwork season.

One afternoon a Taoseño named *A* walked to a corner of one of his fields to open up the irrigation ditch. Shortly after diverting the water from another field to his own he was accosted by *B*, who informed him somewhat testily that he had not finished irrigating. *A* informed *B* that he had signed up for this time and that he was accompanied by *C*, who would be a witness. *B* argued that he had received prior commitment for the particular block of time for the entire season, and offered to secure witnesses to this effect. Grumbling and muttering, *A* turned away and left, and *B* redirected the water to his own field.

The following day *A* once more returned to the field at about the same time, and again turned on the irrigation water. It was not long before *B* arrived, and this time precipitated a heated argument over respective rights, beginning at the pitch where they had parted ways the previous day. After a few minutes of fruitless contention they stopped arguing; *B* simply changed the watercourse while *A* watched, glowering. *A* changed it back and then told *B* he had better leave things as they were or they would come to blows. After hesitating for a moment, *B* stomped off.

The issue did not end here. The two parties to the conflict had previously been governor and lieutenant-governor in the pueblo. *A* was a son of the shaman whose family had earlier built up the opposition to the peyote boys and their families. *B*'s family had been on the other side of that controversy. Certain members of his family had also come under censure later for acting as informants

for Elsie Clews Parsons after that dispute was terminated. Both
A and B could gain adherents from parties who had suffered griev-
ances during the earlier conflicts. It is significant that this dispute
over irrigation rights was not brought to the "ditch boss," whose
function it is to regulate water resources. This would have been
normal procedure; and if the conflict could not be resolved at this
level, recourse could then be had to the Council. As it happened,
the ditch boss was a supporter of the powerful chief of the Big
Earrings kiva, a ranking member of the northern moiety. (Ceremonial and political functions are distributed not only among the
several kivas, of which there are now six, but also between dual
divisions consisting of three kiva societies each and labeled "north"
and "south" or "male" and "female.") Although the ditch boss was
relatively young (in his early forties) and inexperienced, both
parties tacitly agreed that he was not likely to judge the matter
impartially, especially since B belonged to a group that opposed
the kiva chief in question. In the end A and B worked things out
on their own. B gradually ceased to irrigate for as long a time as
he felt he was entitled to; A irrigated less frequently and arrived
a little later. But even this mode of handling the matter was to
some degree an abandonment of a central cooperative activity in
pueblo life.

THE CRISIS AT THE BRIDGE

In the spring of 1949 a group of Taos veterans decided to call a
public meeting to discuss the merits of setting up a training program in agriculture and the manual arts in Taos in connection with
the G.I. Bill of Rights. The veterans decided to hold the meeting
at the Taos Day School, and spread the announcement of the day
and hour by word of mouth. At the same time, after some discussion they decided to invite the superintendent of the United
Pueblo Agency in Albuquerque to attend. The superintendent,
unaware of the train of events in the village, wired the governor
his acceptance. The governor at once summoned the Council. At
the urging of the head of the Big Earrings kiva, the most powerful
of the kiva chiefs, the Council took a firm stand against allowing
the proposed meeting to be held at the schoolhouse. No room was

left for compromise, such as holding a meeting away from the pueblo, either outside the wall or in the town of Taos. As Fenton put it, the decision "that there would be no meeting off the pueblo or on the school grounds or in its assembly, denied the possibility of summoning the pueblo to meet outside the wall and ignored the fact that the pueblo has no community hall" (1957, p. 336). A meeting would be sanctioned only if it took place at the governor's house in the pueblo. The veterans rejected this ultimatum, which they felt would inhibit the free discussion they had in mind, and decided to proceed with the original plan.

Charges and countercharges were made for several days. On the day set for the meeting, the superintendent of the Agency arrived at the hotel in Taos, where he was met by the head religious chief and the governor and advised not to come to the pueblo. He rejected this advice, upon which the war chief and his aides stationed a force of men at the bridge leading to the pueblo, to prevent movement either in or out. The veterans could not call a meeting in the town of Taos, nor could the superintendent enter the pueblo without a show of force. As a result of this stalemate no further action was taken; later in the evening, after several futile attempts to assemble interested parties at a neutral place, the superintendent returned to Albuquerque.

THE ROLE OF EXTERNAL FORCES

In effect, the veterans justified consulting the superintendent on the ground that a traditional right of calling for public assembly to discuss a controversial issue had been denied. Actually, however, all available case materials strongly indicate this right had pertained in the past exclusively to disputes within the Council; in the rare cases where unanimity was not achieved, the Council would customarily assemble the people for a final resolution. The incident was a departure from precedent in another way as well.

Individuals and groups had appealed to the Pueblo Agency on other occasions, especially in the past twenty-five years, but this marked the first time that the superintendent had actually been invited to participate in a dispute at the pueblo.

Not only was an agent of the American government involved in this dispute, but various other people from outside the pueblo took an active part. The newspaper at the town of Taos editorialized strongly in support of the Council, and a nonpueblo veterans' group backed the pueblo veterans on the basis of civil rights, democracy, and the right of assembly. Local artists with whom some of the veterans had studied on the G.I. bill expressed support for their views in the local newspaper, while other artists supported the Council. This outside interference undercut the authority of the traditional pueblo officials even further.

As in the Ayudha Puja incident, all attempts at arbitration failed, and the controversy over rights was never resolved. Since it involved virtually all able-bodied adults in the pueblo, the round of daily activities returned to a recognizable routine, but it has never returned to what had theretofore been considered "normal." For example, summons to all communal activities, including ceremonial dances, are usually made by the governor, the war chief, and their aides; this includes announcing who is to participate in ceremonial dances, when they are to attend practice sessions in respective kivas, and so on. It has become increasingly difficult to impose and enforce penalties for nonparticipation in these activities, with the result that several ceremonials of the annual round have not been presented regularly, and those that remain in the curtailed annual cycle are often criticized for lack of proper attention to detail and reverential attitudes. Younger men are responding less and less frequently to requests to serve as apprentices to civil officers, almost a prerequisite to any attempts at innovation. Village-wide cooperation has become practically impossible to secure on almost any other conflict-laden issue, whether it be the storing of grain in a community granary until market prices are favorable, agreement on irrigation schedules, or the buying of farm machinery for collective use.

THE MEMBERSHIP OF DISPUTING GROUPS

The alignment of contestants in the climactic bridge-incident controversy was considerably more complex than one might imagine. Conservatives vs. progressives, councilors vs. veterans, is only part of the story. Past relations among councilors at the time of the controversy played a part in their choice of sides. Certain younger and newer members of the Council, as well as (or including) parties to the earlier peyote crisis, did not fully support the attempt at monolithic action by the older leaders, and especially by the chief of the Big Earrings kiva. Families with veteran sons were in conflict with families with no veteran sons; and where such differently constituted families were united by marriage, tensions tended to disrupt normal relations among affinals. Among the veterans, also, there were dissenters. Some of these men refused to participate in the actions that led to the crisis at the bridge, and a few sided with the councilors.

The attempt to close the ranks of the Council in opposing the meeting called by the veterans was pursued in traditional fashion. The dominant hierarchy, consisting of the priestly heads of the four kivas and the Cacique, called a meeting of the Council, largely at the urging of the Big Earrings kiva chief. (This chief was in effect the headman of the village, initiating virtually all the controlling actions within the politico-religious system.) Only about 60 per cent of the Council members were invited to attend, however. Invitations were issued only to those who could be expected to approve the majority opinion, unanimity being a necessary condition if any action were to be taken. All those invited had been supporters of the chief of Big Earrings kiva over the preceding several years.

The Big Earrings chief also exerted control over a number of younger men and their families by dispensing favors to them—for example, appointing them as aides to civil officers—in return for which they participated fully in the round of public ceremonials, at the expense of occupational opportunities outside the pueblo that were economically far more rewarding. Headmen could not exert pressure by promising economic rewards, as in Namhalli, because the agricultural lands, although not equally divided, nevertheless required for their exploitation only the labor force of nuclear families. However, families not having at least one male and one female child over the age of thirteen and farming parcels over five acres need help during periods of intensive effort—especially the planting and harvesting of maize. This help may come from certain kindred of the same generation as Ego and/or one generation removed. But when no such kinsmen are available, helpers must be hired for pay, a practice which has occurred with increasing frequency in the last two generations.

The promoters of the veterans' rehabilitation program at Taos were generally delinquent in community service of both kinds. The dominant power elements in the Council simply threw out the veterans' petition to apply for aid from the State Veterans Administration, arguing that younger men had no right even to submit such a petition until they had been properly initiated in the kivas. This initiation involved service of the kinds mentioned above, and implied therefore a long period of socialization by the religiously indoctrinated. According to traditional ideology at Taos, anyone has the right to bring petitions before the Council. The "reading" of this principle, as reflected in the Council's decision at the time of crisis we are considering, was a special one and not universally shared.

It is apparent that antecedent conflicts of several kinds between individuals lay behind the actual membership in the two factions to the dispute. Taos is a less differentiated community than Namhalli: one does not find great diversity in disputants' origins or vast divergence from traditional organizational alignments. On the other hand, membership in the factions did not tend to follow simple lines. Instead, fathers and sons, brothers and brothers, kin members of the same kiva, and affinally linked families were as likely as not to be found on opposite sides. Some officials who had several times in the past clashed with other officials in the Council also took opposing sides in the latest conflict. The lieutenant-governor, a governor who had resigned earlier in the year, and an ex-governor joined the veterans' group. Still others vacillated, or assumed a neutral stance.

Two final observations emerge from an analysis of events preceding the dispute over the veterans' meeting at the pueblo. In the first place, the issues that generated conflict could not from the anthropologist's viewpoint be said to have in themselves threatened either the survival or the integrity of the pueblo. Purification of the water supply, for example, the introduction of electricity, and the improvement of road access to and from the community have been accomplished at other, even more conservative, pueblos with little or none of the heated controversy observed at Taos. Probably no one in the pueblo was in principle opposed even to a consideration of special educational measures requested by the veterans. This and other conflicts described above might well have been handled by traditionally available mechanisms. From this point of view these conflicts might be considered trivial.

Second, and related to this factor, no new coping technique, such as arbitration or creating a system of majority rule rather than rule by unanimous consent within the Council, was ever suggested to handle these new problems. It might be added that no one ever disputed the basic goal orientation of the pueblo as an organization. Despite all their frustrations, the young men proclaimed in almost every other statement that they wished to be Taos Indians.[1] What was wanted was not a revolutionary change in the structure of the community but a return to coping procedures already available within it. These included (1) a genuine alternation of power holders among the kivas; (2) public hearings on issues that involved significant elements of the population; and (3) adhering in most issues to the rule of unanimity, but limiting invitations to Council meetings to those likely to agree.

BACKGROUND OF THE SCHOOL-MEETING INCIDENT

The worldwide influenza epidemic toward the end of World War I reduced the population of Taos pueblo by several hundred.

---

[1] The dissidents did finally come to feel so alienated from the decision-making group that they formed a People's Party, in 1947 or thereabouts, which sought certain major transformations in the political process of the pueblo. The members of this party requested, among other things, a written charter or constitution, a voice in the choosing of the Council, and more efficient controls over the allocation and use of pueblo funds. It is significant that these requests were tendered to the United Pueblo Agency director and not to the Council itself.

Thereafter an upward rise already apparent before the turn of the century was resumed. Agricultural productivity, upon which maintenance of the ideological system depends, rose with a somewhat more intensive use of land and increased use of fertilizers; but given the short growing season and the pueblo's fixed boundaries, the rise in productivity could not keep pace with rate of population growth. By 1949 the pueblo bought nearly half its food with wages earned by working outside the village (Siegel, 1949, pp. 567–68). Families with very large plots could still spend their time in the traditional manner; but more and more Taoseños were obliged to seek work outside the village.

During World War II a substantial number of young men— more than one-tenth the total population—were drafted into the armed forces. The hierarchy at that time elected not to invoke special privileges as an agricultural population, which would have granted deferred status to otherwise eligible draftees, on the assurance by draft officials that the young men would be returned to the community after termination of hostilities. Certain important village-wide ceremonial activities were curtailed. Taos servicemen established new kinds of relationships, acquired new wants, learned a new system of prescriptions, and experienced relief from traditional demands for extreme control over emotional expression. The elders were rightly anxious over their ability to reinstitute an accepted long-range deference to adult prestige roles among the returnees. Upon their return to the pueblo many young men found themselves insufficiently indoctrinated and with too slender a record of local service to be considered for positions of secular and sacred authority.

Like Namhalli, Taos experienced an increase in employment opportunities outside the community; unlike Namhalli, it experienced a population increase with definite restrictions on internal productive potential. Whereas Namhalli had long exported and imported marriage partners and coped in an active sense with markets, towns, and cities in its environment, Taos had successfully defended itself against alternatives and pressures from these sources. The curtailment of employment and market opportunities created stresses in the Indian village; their expansion created stresses in the pueblo.

Under these circumstances conflicts in Taos intensified and increased in number. They were not restricted to the hierarchy and the "boys," but entered into virtually every customary relationship between individuals. No one proposed that the pueblo reconsider its traditional ways, that it establish increased links with external markets, that it give some thought to converting a subsistence base to surplus production of cash crops. No one suggested that the old techniques for ensuring cooperation and handling disputes were inadequate, or that new solutions were required. Traditional mechanisms continued to work in some cases, but the authorities were driven increasingly to such stern methods as summary arrest and jailing, at the expense of such once-favored methods as suasion, the leveling of fines, or the imposing of special community tasks.

VARIETIES OF CONFLICT

After World War II, several cases were reported in which unmarried sons refused to assist with agricultural work. A man in such a position might do one of two things: ask a kinsman to take his place at times when extra hands are needed, or hire labor from outside the pueblo. It is considered unfortunate to be forced to resort to either of these alternatives, especially the hiring of labor. Most sons establish separate residences when they marry, but continue to assist the natal household and each other's households. Family members of several independent households thus constitute a first circle of collaborative effort.

Beyond this group any individual can enter into reciprocal aid relationships with a network of agnatic or uterine kindred that in practice extends collaterally two degrees. The principle that tends to govern the choice of kinsmen in Taos is reciprocal need. Six men in the summer of 1947 refused to respond to a request for field help, arguing that they could not leave their jobs outside the village. Until that time it was customary on such occasions to leave a job with or without notice and return to it as soon as possible, a practice that scarcely commended itself to Anglo employers. By refusing to respond, the six men contributed to asymmetry in the service exchange system. They served notice that the normal modes of collaboration had ceased to operate in respect to an important activity, and thus directly threatened the basic authority system.

Divorce is rare in Taos; even separations are infrequent, and they are disapproved as a step in the handling of domestic altercations. In 1947 there was only one divorced couple in the community. The following year the Anglo wife of another Taos man left the pueblo and later obtained a divorce in California. At this time the governor, at the behest of the chief kiva head, demanded that any non-Indian wife (there was one English war bride as well as the Anglo wife) and all nonpueblo husbands leave the pueblo, the latter because they presumably did not have sufficient training to participate in the ceremonial round. It appears that arbitrary annulments of this kind, imposed from above, have been decreed on other occasions in the past when the hierarchy felt it necessary to consolidate its position.

It has been difficult to obtain systematic evidence on the facts of marital dispute—its basic causes, its incidence, and the ways of handling it (for example, separation, reconciliation, mediation by kinsmen or by other villages whence wives have come). In view of Taoseños' aversion to any public airing of quarrels and conflicts, the extent to which husband-wife disputes become public knowledge and the subject of much gossip is in itself a crude indicator of the weakening of mechanisms of control. Gossip at Taos is a keen defensive weapon against nonconformity. During the postwar period, however, what troubled people most was that such gossip often failed to have the proper shaming effect.

In one case, a wife complained bitterly when her husband used a substantial part of her earnings to buy liquor. When complaints failed, she took her troubles to her parents, who threatened to have the husband arrested by the war chief unless he behaved more responsibly. The husband responded by leaving home for about ten days. Finally he returned home, but very soon he had fallen into his old ways. He took to beating his wife, and on one occasion the wife's father made good his threat and had the son-in-law jailed for misuse of domestic funds. The relations between the two progressively worsened. This progression of events further rendered more difficult the normal relations between other affinals among the kindred, so that cooperation in the preparation and giving of feasts on ceremonial occasions broke down.

8. On the Study of Conflict

Since the symbol systems and patterns of behavior of Namhalli and Taos are different, there are certain problems in comparing them. In Taos a verbal conflict symbolizes an almost intolerable level of divisiveness; at Namhalli an apparently equal level of disruption is indicated by the imminence of physical violence. Conflict at Namhalli appears to have reached an acute stage following the end of World War II, but to have tapered off as patterns of stress changed. Taos appears to have been less constrained by stress than Namhalli, but it faced stresses of longer duration that neither forced an acceleration of conflict nor permitted it to be snuffed out. Factionalist dispute tends to last as long as it continues to be supported by an appropriate balance of inside and outside forces. The rate and disruptiveness of factionalist dispute may well, as for other processes, depend upon the conditions within which it takes place. If the wind is high, the flame burns faster.

Taos and Namhalli differ in the way groups are formed, in the way conflicts occur and are arbitrated, and in the frequency and disruptive effects of conflicts. Similarities between the communities are also numerous. In both communities, conflict made it much harder to carry out normal problem-solving activities or to develop new solutions to new problems. Such everyday problems as establishing boundaries of fields in Namhalli or allocating irrigation water in both villages suddenly became of focal interest, generating major conflicts that consumed the time and energy of the community. Both communities had water purification problems, and neither was able to improve its access road. Vital ceremonies could not be performed, and a united front could not be presented to the outside world. In both communities, desperation led to the un-precedented step of seeking outside assistance in conflict resolution. In both cases, despite humiliation and loss, outside intervention failed to resolve the conflict.

In both cases, the problem-solving capabilities of the organization may have declined for other reasons—e.g., because there were fewer problems to be solved, or different kinds of problems—but there is no evidence to this effect. Persons familiar with the communities continually emphasize the need for strong united action. There appears to be a feeling tone characteristic of factionalist dispute:

Just so, conflict within a closely knit group often enough grows beyond the extent justified by its occasion and by the interest to the group immediately attendant on this occasion, for, in addition, this conflict is associated with the feeling that the discord is not a matter only of the two parties but of the group as a whole. Each party fights, as it were, in the name of the whole group and must hate in its adversary not only its own enemy but at the same time the enemy of the higher sociological unit. [Simmel, 1955, p. 50]

Again: "Each group feels itself the champion of a righteous cause. Each sees the other as a force destructive of the values which it cherishes." (The Inquiry, 1929, p. 3.) In both Namhalli and Taos the same violent accusations are leveled against the opposing side, and against the people as a whole. External threats and problems are dismissed as insignificant while people devote their attention to character assassination and the rhetoric of distrust.

Another attribute of factionalism is the tendency for disputes to come to a head over seemingly trivial incidents. At Namhalli, the apparent cause of the Ayudha Puja incident was a question concerning the proper height of the deity's carriage and the propriety of cutting off the branch of a tree. In Taos, disputes centered about proper dress or holding dances at the school. The apparent triviality of such a large proportion of factional disputes is consistent with the idea that the conflict actually concerns the desire to compel other members of the organization to abide by the decisions of some particular group. The goal is to "bring down" the opposing side. Defeat or victory on any particular issue is far more important than the issue itself.

Not only are the incidents around which factionalist disputes are generated often trivial, but they may also arise out of disputes that are not ordinarily threats to solidarity. Ordinary family quarrels have a tendency to snowball, so that what starts out as a quarrel between husband and wife, or a quarrel between brothers, comes to involve more and more people. The conflict between *A* and *B* at Taos over the distribution of irrigation water is a case in point. Groups form on the basis of enmity as much as on the basis of any need for cooperation. Anyone who is an enemy of *B* is a friend of *A*, and even those who previously were enemies of both must now choose or forgo the pleasure of revenge. By the same rule, friends of *A* become enemies of *B*.

We are brought, now, inexorably to the fact that the sides or factions which participate in factionalist dispute are likely to be amorphous. Pocock (1957) finds that the membership of factions is "determined by the precise circumstances of their occurrence," and that there seems to be no structural necessity underlying factionalist alignments. Speaking of Gujerat, he defines factions as follows (p. 296): "To sum up so far: when we speak of factions we have in mind conflicting groups conceived as parts of a whole; the conflict is not an internal necessity of this whole but tends to disrupt it; factions are not permanent groups, and their membership is determined by the circumstances in which they occur; factions are composite." As it happens, factions in Taos appear to be far less amorphous than factions in Namhalli. Even for Namhalli, there are some grounds for describing the factions as "progressive" and "conservative" (Beals, 1954), and it is possible to account for some of the membership in each of the two factions in terms of caste, family, and neighborhood alignments. Perhaps the key point is that factionalist dispute tends to shatter traditional alignments and exploit the internal weaknesses of existing families and subgroups. If factionalist disputes merely reflected existing alignments, they would offer relatively few problems to those traditionally charged with adjudicating disputes. A conflict is usually the same old people arguing about the same old thing or new people arguing about something new. In Taos, a relatively well-organized controversy between progressives and conservatives over peyote gradually became diffuse and amorphous. Oscar Lewis (1954) suggests the same movement of events in his description of a North Indian village. From another point of view, if it is argued that schismatic factionalism involves two well-organized factions, it follows that disputes can be resolved only by the leaders of the two factions. These all-powerful leaders are likely to decide either to bury the hatchet or to dissolve the organization. Where factions are amorphous and unstable, as in pervasive factionalism, the leader's position depends upon his success in putting down the opposition. He cannot play the role of peacemaker until all the individual enmities that form the basis of the factional alignments have been settled.

The final major characteristic of factionalism in Namhalli and Taos, then, is its pervasive nature. In both cases conflict was rife at the community level and at sublevels within the community, and in both cases pre-existing kinship ties and psychological attitudes afforded no easy clues to faction membership. Indeed, different pueblos developed factionalism along different lines. For example, Whitman encountered religious conflict in San Ildefonso and many factions in Santa Clara (1947), whereas French found factionalism to have developed around a political schism in Isleta (1948). Why should such otherwise similar communities be divided by conflict in such different ways? May it not be simply that, once a factionalist dispute begins to develop, the faction leaders attempt to claim the support of existing organizations and viewpoints even though the organizations are divided and the viewpoints not uniformly held?

STRESSES AND STRAINS

The present theory argues that factionalist dispute comes from the interaction between internal strains and external stresses. This means that whatever the degree of strain in a community, divisiveness develops only where there is also an appropriate variety of

stress. In both Namhalli and Taos, as we have seen, a single concept of leadership and authority was generalized through a number of critical role relationships; in effect, the community was
regarded as a family and the leader of the community as a family
head. The strength of this pattern is evident; its weakness lies
in the fact that the weakening of any one position of authority
involves the weakening of all. Both communities emphasized
harmony and unanimity. Both were "big, happy families." Both
communities also attached great importance to cooperative ceremonials and unanimity in reaching decisions, and both sharply
defined the rights, duties, and reciprocal obligations of community
members in such a way as to inhibit change in the distribution of
goods and services. Both attempted to solve problems by invoking
tradition. In both, the mechanisms for legislation were slow and
cumbersome. In a sense, the traditions of both communities were
effective. For centuries no one dreamed that stresses might arise
that would threaten even basic beliefs about the nature of things.

In time, however, Namhalli and Taos were subjected to stresses
that lacked the character of visible threat yet sharply limited the
freedom of action of the community and acted selectively against
the village leadership—punishing authorities, rewarding subordinates. In both cases, the stress involved the introduction of radically new values and beliefs from a variety of sources. In both
cases, the stress operated on pre-existing strains in the traditional
patterns of authority and conflict resolution to produce factionalist dispute, not just at the community level but in vital dyadic
relationships such as husband-wife and parent-child. This is perhaps as much as we know. If the foregoing descriptions of Namhalli and Taos raise more problems than they resolve, that is all
to the good. The study of conflict requires far more data than are
currently available, and it requires that such data be collected in
terms of some kind of systematic theory.

DISTRIBUTION OF FACTIONALIST DISPUTE

How common is factionalist dispute? No doubt, as has often
been assumed, conflict is universal in human societies, but what

kinds of conflict are we talking about? What occasions generate conflicts? There is a great difference, after all, between competition, regulated conflict, and factionalist dispute. Unfortunately, if we define factionalist dispute as a naturally occurring process involving an unregulated exchange of oppositions that is disruptive of normal group processes, we find the anthropological literature remarkably unhelpful. Despite the prevalence of assumptions that conflict is functional or dysfunctional, most accounts of conflict fail to indicate clearly its effect on the group within which it occurs.[1] That a conflict is good for management or serves the cause of imperialism is surely, if not irrelevant, ancillary.

We are not certain how disruptiveness is to be measured, but certainly it must involve an inability to persist in old ways or to adopt new ones. In many settings factionalism occurs in some organizations but not in others; this raises the hope that, for a particular region or set of communities, a standard of normal functioning can be established. Certainly, where crops are irrigated, we can expect that water will be regulated; where there is marriage, we can expect that the divorce rate will be reasonably stable. To measure disruption, of course, we need not only a standard but a way of measuring changes over time. We might start by comparing the expectations of community members—e.g., about cooperation—with the realization of them in practice, but this, too, raises difficulties. In any case, the existing accounts of conflict rarely discuss its impact except in general terms.

Usually, in addition, there is no detailed contextualization of the conflict. Historical antecedents are lacking, even in the form of myth and legend, and although factionalist dispute or some-

---

[1] At times, even when an attempt is being made to describe what has been gained and lost in the course of a conflict, the bias in favor of functionalism is so strong as to lead to a complete suppression of any information concerning disruptive aspects. Firth (1957, pp. 293–94) goes so far as to suggest that factional conflict is designed to let off steam, to "provide a kind of 'war game' for the energies of those who might otherwise be engaged in the more responsible control of public affairs," but he also recognizes "the negative aspects of factions, their turbulence, the unscrupulousness of their methods, their disregard of communal responsibility, their expression of disruptive forces in the community."

thing like it can be seen to accompany some kinds of rapid cultural change, the external influences involved are inadequately described. The possibility that factionalist dispute might emerge cyclically as a part of the normal functioning of a society cannot be explored because there are few descriptions of such cycling. Finally, there are problems of scale. Much of the literature concerns tribes, islands, or other entities too large to study in our terms. Some writers on conflict fail to define the term; others define it ambiguously or too narrowly. Often one cannot determine whether they are discussing overt or psychological conflict. Others defend particular definitions of such terms as "party" or "faction" far more vigorously than their analyses warrant.

In the literature, the term "factionalism" occurs most frequently in discussions of political parties, industrial settings, villages in India, pueblos in the American Southwest, communities in the United States, American Indian reservations in the United States, and Micronesian islands and villages. Within these categories, factionalism, insofar as it can be identified as factionalist dispute, does not occur within every community or organization, nor is it consistently pervasive or schismatic, nor is it present at the same time in different communities. For example, Picuris Pueblo lacks any form of party conflict or factionalism, Taos inclines strongly toward pervasive factionalism, and other pueblos (cf. French, 1948), incline toward schismatic factionalism.

Party factions appear to be universal in the larger and anthropologically attractive villages both in India and transplanted overseas. In the village described by Lewis (1958) parties are stable and patterns of conflict resolution clearly established. In a study of thirty villages of Mysore State (Beals, 1965a), it was found that party conflict occurred in most villages of more than 500 persons possessing either a single dominant caste or two competing dominant castes. In two cases schismatic factionalism appears to have developed, possibly because of modern influences. Srinivas' account of conflict in Rampur (1955) indicates the presence of party conflict, a distinction evident in the presence of a strongly dominant headman and a tendency to unite in the face of outside threat.

In Rajasthan, Carstairs (1957, p. 43) finds a feud between factions: "It has gone on to quarrels, fights, law-suits, 'rigging' of the village panchayat elections—and it seems to gather momentum as it goes." Lewis mentions a similar tendency toward a transition from party conflict toward factionalist dispute. Nicholas (1963) describes how the clique groups of a Bengal village, which he calls factions, are allied to form parties. Despite incomplete data, it is apparent that party conflict, schismatic factionalism, and pervasive factionalism all occur in India. Perhaps because the Indian environment encourages community studies, more studies of conflict are available from India than from any other part of the world.

Micronesia, considering its small population, contributes heavily to the literature on divisiveness. The island of Majuro, which has been described by Tobin (1953), seems to represent schismatic factionalism (p. 18):

The atoll community organization has been seriously disrupted by the dispute. This disruption is eloquently symbolized by a sailboat which is rotting on the beach at Majuro Island. This sailboat, the "Marjana," a forty-two footer, was given to the atoll council in 1948 by the Civil Administrator. The boat was operated for almost a year until its leaky condition forced the council to beach it. A dispute over title and the lack of cooperation between the two groups has prevented the repair of this boat, which was and is badly needed in the economic life of the atoll. The "Marjana," a silent symbol of mutual distrust and uncooperativeness, rots away on the Majuro Island beach today.

At the time Tobin made his observations, disruption had not involved the community school or dispensary, although work on school construction was halted for a time by conflict. Spoehr, writing at an earlier date (1949), observed cleavage and conflict on Majuro, but an absence of physical violence. He found instances of cooperation between the two factions, but he also found tendencies toward receiving and entertaining visitors and celebrating festive occasions separately (pp. 82–90).

Vidich (1949), in his discussion of political factionalism on Palau, attributes the conflict to "the interaction of the foreign and indigenous money systems, changes in the occupational structure, the shift from a subsistence to a surplus economy, the introduction of the concept of private property, the industrialization of Palau, and changes in the functioning of the exchange and contributory customs" (p. 120). Useem (1949) found that Palau had adjusted to changing conditions with little disorganization, but on one island, Angaur, he noted some disharmony (p. 7):

For three decades the villages have disputed among themselves the distribution of the available land, and this controversy still continues. The full scope of the issues is too involved to be given in detail here, for they include not merely questions of land rights, but also the political relationships between the villages, old feuds between clans, and a new struggle for power within the elite class.

In describing the Plateau Tonga in Africa, Elizabeth Colson (1959, p. 100) writes: "Under pressure of the rains the Tonga did not attempt to unite in a common defense of their country. During such respites as they had from external foes they continued their internal feuds and fought against each other. By 1890 they were a broken and beaten people." Gluckman (1941, pp. 54–55) writes of the Zulu: "Divisions of each large group into political groups and opposed groups with conflicting ideals and interests act to weaken each group within itself and to lessen the main opposition." In another article, Gluckman (1939) suggests the development of pervasive factionalism among the Zulu: "Open disintegration" is attributed to the British invasion (p. 157), and "Personal and tribal quarrels, previously restrained by the national cohesion, broke out in open conflicts" (p. 158). He concludes (p. 168):

Conflicts which cannot be resolved by a return to the original equilibrium inevitably produce changes in the pattern and its parts: and this happened in the period before the formation of the Zulu nation and has been happening since the establishment of White rule. Despite all attempted resolutions the central conflict persists and increases, and every temporary adjustment engenders further conflicts between persisting and evolved parts in a new pattern.

Balandier (1955) compares the Fang of Gabon and the Ba-uongo of the French Congo, and concludes that internal conflicts have hindered the Fang's adaptation.

In the Middle Eastern village of Hadeth El-Jobbé, Toufic (1958) finds a developing schism that prevents any relationship of exchange with the outside world. The conflicting groups are described as forming around single leaders (p. 63), and the social strata or cleavages are described as "vacillating" or "changing order" (p. 116). The lines of force are not parallel or perpendicular, the choices are multiple, the systems fluctuate; only certain poles stay in one place for long periods (p. 118). Whether Toufic's account describes party conflict or schismatic or pervasive factionalism is not clear, for he concludes with the observation that "solidarity is manifested spontaneously under quite different circumstances; in festivals, dances and recreations, everybody is in unison" (p. 118).

For the North American Indians there are a number of descriptions of various kinds of factionalism. Nicholas (1963) has contributed a detailed discussion of party conflict, fission, clique group formation, and factionalist dispute among the Iroquois, but he says nothing about the extent to which the various conflicts were disruptive. French's description of Isleta Pueblo as an example of "social pathology" fits the definition of factionalist dispute. At Isleta, "Differences tend to increase with time, and the breach remains open until the issue disappears, or one group abandons its position, or a settlement is effected by an outside agency like the Indian Service" (1948, p. 38). French's account has little to say about the causes of factionalism at Isleta beyond attributing it to modern pressures. Elsewhere, Spicer finds "political discord and factions among Arizona Yaquis" (1940, p. 149).

Several of the groups described in Linton's *Acculturation in Seven American Indian Tribes* (1940) appear to possess varieties of divisiveness. The White Knife Shoshone and the Southern Ute are described as having two factions. The Fox are described as having "a long history of internal dissension" (p. 310). In her description of the Teton Dakota, Esther Goldfrank (1943) suggests that such changes as the introduction of liquor and an unequal distribution of wealth, together with the removal of outside threats, caused an increase in ingroup violence during the first half of the nineteenth century. When outside threats reappeared, ingroup violence declined. When peace was declared, it increased again (p. 80): "For thirty years, increasing emphasis had been placed upon tribal cooperation and familial solidarity. Yet once the external threat was removed and acute internal situations again developed, the precepts of the recent past were quickly over-ridden. The Teton reverted to the violent behavior so common before 1850." Vanstone, in his description of Point Hope, a community free of divisive conflicts, indicates that factionalist disputes over religious matters are common in other Eskimo communities (1962, p. 157). Chance compares two Eskimo communities, one of which has strikingly more conflict than the other (1960, pp. 1028–44).

For other countries and periods, one can find only occasional mentions of various kinds of divisiveness. Pierson (1948) notes conflict between religious sects and struggles between political factions in a Japanese community; conflict is reported to occur not in terms of personalities, but in terms of old versus modern ways of thinking. Becker (1931), writing about the Renaissance, suggests that unrest was caused by the breakdown of isolated communities, a consequence of the Crusades. Brown and Shepherd (1956) report a case of schismatic factionalism from a research laboratory, the result being a number of resignations. Nehnevajsa 1957) reports from the Soviet Union a general tendency toward factionalism as a result, among other things, of the *success* ethic of the Bolsheviks. Here, factionalism is attributed to what sounds very much like the dyadic contract of Foster (1961). The proposition that factionalist dispute tends to be absent where the dyadic contract is dominant merits close study (Nehnevajsa, 1957; Foster, 1961, pp. 1190–91). According to Nehnevajsa, factions develop as networks of persons with similar interests; conflict breaks out when supposedly trustworthy persons fail to perform successfully.

One of the most detailed accounts of schismatic factionalism occurs in Redfield's study of Chan Kom (1934). Chan Kom's disputes, like Namhalli's, were largely due to rapid cultural change, and ended when the village's adjustment to the urban world had been completed. A cleavage between the Ceme and Pat families, which had existed from the founding of the community, had been controlled and was not disruptive. When Protestant missionaries intervened, the Protestant Pat family became dominant within the cult, and the Catholic Cemes withdrew. This led to an open break. Protestants refused to contribute labor for a Catholic church. The elders of the two factions struck each other, and the Protestants were thrown in jail. Under pressure from the Cemes, some of the Pat families withdrew and tried to cause outlying hamlets to secede from Chan Kom. The Protestant influence and the attempt to continue the battle on different terms both suggest that something is involved other than a normal fission mechanism. Further, regarding Tepoztlan, Lewis (1951, p. 251) remarks: "Political parties as such exist only in name. Instead there are poorly organized and undisciplined political factions whose members are united more by personal ties of friendship or kinship than by common political ideology."

In industrialized societies, detailed reports have been made of conflicts in local communities (Coleman, 1957; The Inquiry, 1929), labor unions (Dubin, 1960; Kornhauser, *et al.*, 1954), and political parties, and more recently in groups concerned with civil rights for Negroes and university students. The prevalence of party conflict and factionalist dispute in all modern societies is indisputable. Yet what are we to make of this brief review? Very little, it would appear, until we have a meaningful theory of conflict and until we have more detailed cases. It is only a beginning to describe conflict as eufunctional or disruptive, as contributing or not contributing to the maintenance of things as they are. There is empirical justification in the literature for our distinction between disruptive and nondisruptive conflict. It is somewhat more difficult to identify differences between pervasive and schismatic factionalism, though the literature amply demonstrates the existence of a more pervasive variety of factionalism than is found in such well-organized schisms as Pat vs. Ceme. We must go much deeper. Taos and Namhalli are by no means unique, nor are their problems encountered only in agricultural communities. To understand these problems better, social scientists must devise a meaningful typology of conflict.

THEORIES OF CONFLICT

Most ethnographic descriptions of factionalist dispute and party conflict contain relatively little theoretical material, and most theories of conflict have been hampered by an excessive emphasis on equilibrium and functionalism. Functionalism tends to deal with static social structures rather than dynamic social processes, and to emphasize the constructive and beneficial nature of conflict. A considerable effort has been devoted to defining the term "faction." Some writers say that factions are fluid and unstable groups in conflict, others that factions are stable groups in conflict (Firth, 1957; Pocock, 1957; Nicholas, 1963; Boissevain, 1964). The second definition is hard to sustain. If factions are groups or near-groups involved in conflict, it follows that they must encounter defeat and emerge victorious; and if the conflict is to continue, there must be means of recruiting new sources of support following a defeat or of losing support following a victory. Logically, factions cannot be stable groups, although their component cliques and families may be.

Firth (1957) suggests that factions contain elements of a positive character: they help their members achieve their own ends, attain flexibility, and develop moral and social virtues; they mobilize opinion; and they offer alternatives to full-fledged political and social conflict (pp. 293–94). A good, noisy street riot between opposing factions, particularly if it involves much destruction of life and property, may indeed be a blessing in some way or other. It is not clear where anthropological theory enters into this. Whatever the benefits of conflict, should it be accepted that a state of continual and unremitting violence is the proper condition of mankind? We can imagine that a society can have too little conflict or too much conflict. The important question is to determine which kinds of conflict are beneficial or harmful under which kinds of circumstances.

Attempts to reduce conflict groups to rigid social structural categories and to demonstrate, in each case, the functional value of observed conflicts has not brought us a single step closer to a body of theory that would permit prediction of the occurrence of conflict, of its effects, of the persons involved, or of the patterns of escalation that might follow. We do not intend to dismiss the pioneering theoretical work of Simmel (1955) and his successors as unimportant. But Simmel did not provide a truly empirical basis for the study of conflict, or a definition of conflict that could serve as a basis for a continuing scientific dialogue. He grasped the symbolic nature of conflict, but never threw off the structural and eufunctional biases of his times.

SOME MODERN APPROACHES

The modern sociology of conflict had its clearest beginnings in the work of Bateson and Sorokin. It was Bateson (1936) who first attacked the notion that distinctions could be made among economic, structural, sexual, and religious behavior—all categories, as he pointed out, that are artificial constructions of the social scientist. In rejecting the functionalist approach, he directed his attention toward interpersonal relationships (1958 ed., p. 176):

When our discipline is defined in terms of the reactions of an individual to the reactions of other individuals, it is at once apparent that we must regard the relationship between two individuals as liable to alter from time to time, even without disturbance from outside. We have to consider, not only A's reactions to B's behavior, but we must go on to consider how these affect B's later behavior and the effect of this on A.

He goes on to point out that the relationship between two individuals or groups may, then, contain tendencies toward progressive change. Here is a basis for conceiving of conflict as an exchange of oppositions.

A dynamic theory of conflict is foreshadowed in Sorokin's work on revolution (1937). In Sorokin's view, the process of internal disturbances commences with the breakdown of the "crystallized system of relationships" and moves on to outbursts of "confusion, conflict, overt violence" (p. 261). In addition to interpreting conflict as a result of strain, or at least of confusion concerning proper behavior, Sorokin indicates the possibilities of multiple causes of conflict behavior and the source of conflict in both external and internal factors.

Apart from these two men, neither of whom really set out to develop a general theory, no one else attempted a systematic study of intragroup conflict until Turner, whose classic *Schism and Continuity* appeared in 1957. In this work, a concept of strain is clearly developed (p. xvii):

Interwoven with the analysis of structural form I present detailed studies of situations of crisis, which arise periodically in village life. These crises make visible both contradictions between crucial principles governing village social structure, and conflicts between persons and groups in sets of social relations governed by a single principle.

With the concept of the "social drama," Turner rises above functionalism into what might well be called processionalism. The social drama has "processional form" in the sense that it moves through a series of definite stages: the breach of regular norm-governed relations, mounting crisis, the application of redressive mechanisms, and, at last, reintegration or irreparable breach (p. 91).

There are many other important contributions to the theory of conflict besides those cited above. Coser's several works (1956, 1957, 1961) follow through and maintain the tradition of Simmel, and LeVine (1961) offers a variety of theoretical notions that differ from those presented here. In sociology, business administration, and political science, there have been numerous elaborate preliminary studies of conflict, though no well-developed theories.

CONCLUSION

The present work has attempted to sketch some of the main outlines of a theory of conflict. After defining conflict as an exchange of oppositions, and distinguishing between covert and overt conflict, we indicated three major dimensions for a classification of conflict: the level of sociocultural integration (i.e., the type of group or relationship) affected, the degree to which the conflict is disruptive of ongoing group processes or is so regarded, and the extent to which conflicts are schismatic or pervasive. These dimensions may prove to have important consequences. We have considered the severity of conflict to be culturally relative. Perhaps, although we doubt it, such things as violence, physical injury, and murder can be defined as cultural universals. Styles of adjudication and types of conflict-resolving mechanisms may have an important influence in determining the course of disputes, and might therefore serve as a basis for classification.

In discussing the immediate circumstances that result in the emergence of conflict, we have concentrated upon stress and strain. We have asserted with some other theorists, but not all, that conflict arises out of situations in which proper actions are not specified or not made desirable. In discussing strain, we have pointed to faults of prediction arising from incongruous or unrealistic relationships with the environment, and to faults of structure arising within and between both value-belief and social structures. We have ignored personal strategies, fatigue, hot weather, and the like, and concentrated on what we take to be the basic factors leading to conflicts, notably patterns of leadership and authority. In many circumstances there are alternatives to conflict that may be initiated by virtually the same set of circumstances that in another place or time leads to conflict. These alternatives probably include withdrawal or fission, and the development of fantasy solutions.

Almost nothing is known about the actual processes involved in the unfolding of particular disputes. Presumably, for different groups there are different ways of recognizing, classifying, and defining disputes. There must be particular ways of involving additional persons and subgroups or seeking out intervention, or other processes of settlement and reconciliation. Perhaps there are ways of breaking off a conflict without appealing to third parties. Any given variety of dispute presumably offers several pathways and branches along which those involved may move in the hope of achieving their particular ends. The meaning and implications of particular gestures and phrases can be established by studying their use within particular disputes and in different disputes.

There are appropriate responses when one is told to "shut up," struck across the face with a glove, or accused of being a "goat" or a "widow's son."

Disputes have a variety of outcomes. Description of these outcomes as functional or dysfunctional in a general way contributes very little to the understanding of them. The victor may or may not receive the spoils; the loser may be richly indemnified. The group as a whole may derive great pleasure and amusement from the episode, or it may take twenty years to heal the resulting breach. In the description of outcomes, the most significant step forward would be to describe some.

This book has dealt with divisiveness, with conflict occurring within organizations. The relationships between such internal conflicts and conflicts occurring between groups are not known. If war is conflict that takes place without rules and in the absence of third parties, war may well be basically different in nature from other conflicts. Even so, there is much of interest to be learned about divisiveness, and much that a knowledge of divisiveness can tell us about other social processes. To this end, let there be proposed a range of theories of conflict and let there be collected much information relevant to the causes, the course, and the concluding stages of divisiveness.

Bibliography

Bibliography

Aberle, David F. 1950. "Shared values in complex societies." *Amer. Soc. Rev.* 15: 495–502.

Adams, John B. 1957. "Culture and conflict in an Egyptian village." *Amer. Anthrop.* 59: 225–335.

Balandier, Georges. 1955. Sociologie actuelle de l'Afrique Noir. Paris: Presses Universitaires de France.

Barnett, Homer G. 1941. "Personal conflict and cultural change." *Social Forces* 20: 160–71.

———. 1949. Palauan society. Eugene: Univ. of Oregon Press.

Bateson, Gregory. 1935. "Culture contact and schismogenesis." *Man* 35: 178–83.

———. 1936. Naven. Cambridge: Cambridge Univ. Press. 2d ed. 1958. Stanford: Stanford Univ. Press.

Beaglehole, Ernest, and Pearl Beaglehole. 1938. Ethnology of Pukapuka. Honolulu: The Bishop Museum.

Beals, Alan R. 1954. "Culture change and social conflict in a South Indian village." Unpublished Ph.D. dissertation, Univ. of California.

———. 1955. "Interplay among factors of change in a Mysore village," in Village India, Memoir No. 83 of the AAA, ed. McKim Marriott. Chicago: Univ. of Chicago Press.

———. 1962. Gopalpur, a South Indian village. New York: Holt, Rinehart, and Winston.

———. 1965. "Crime and conflict in some South Indian villages." Unpublished paper.

Becker, Howard. 1931. "Unrest, culture contact, and release during the Middle Ages and the Renaissance.'" *Sthwst. Social Science Quart.* 12: 143–55.

Boissevain, Jeremy. 1964. "Factions, parties, and politics in a Maltese village." *Amer. Anthrop.* 66: 1275–87.

Bolton, H. E. 1916. "The Espejo expedition, 1582–83," in Spanish exploration in the Southwest, 1542–1706. New York: Scribner's.

Brown, Paula, and Clovis Shepherd. 1956. "Factionalism and organization change in a research laboratory." *Social Problems* 3: 235–43.

Carstairs, G. Morris. 1957. The twice-born: A study of a community of high-caste Hindus. London: Hogarth Press.

Chance, Norman. 1960. "Culture change and integration: An Eskimo example." *Amer. Anthrop.* 62: 1028–44.

Clifton, James A. 1963. "Potawatomi Factionalism." Paper read at 62nd annual meeting of the AAA, San Francisco.

Coleman, James S. 1957. Community conflict. Glencoe, Ill.: Free Press.

Colson, Elizabeth. 1953. The Makah Indians, a study of an Indian tribe in modern American society. Minneapolis: Univ. of Minnesota Press.

———. 1959. "The Plateau Tonga of Northern Rhodesia," in Seven tribes of British Central Africa, ed. Elizabeth Colson and Max Gluckman. Manchester: Manchester Univ. Press.

Cornell, John B. 1956. "Matsunagi: The life and social organization of a Japanese mountain community," in Two Japanese villages. Ann Arbor: Univ. of Michigan Press.

Coser, Lewis A. 1956. The functions of social conflict. Glencoe, Ill.: Free Press.

———. 1957. "Social conflict and the theory of social change." *Brit. J. Sociol.* 8: 197–207.

———. 1961. "The termination of conflict." *J. Conflict Resolution* 5: 347–53.

Dozier, Edward P. 1954. The Hopi-Tewa of Arizona. Berkeley: Univ. of California Press.

———. 1962. "Rio Grande Pueblos," in Perspectives in American Indian culture change, ed. E. H. Spicer. Chicago: Univ. of Chicago Press.

Dubin, Robert. 1960. "A theory of conflict and power in union-management relations." *Industrial and Labor Relations* 13: 501–18.

Durkheim, Emile. 1912. Les formes élémentaires de la vie religieuse. Paris: Alcan.

Espinosa, J. M., tr. and ed. 1940. First expedition of Vargas into New Mexico, 1692. Coronado Historical Series, Vol. X. Albuquerque: Univ. of New Mexico Press.

Fallers, Lloyd A. 1956. Bantu bureaucracy. Cambridge: Cambridge Univ. Press.

Fenton, William N. 1955. "Factionalism in American Indian society." *Proceedings of the Fourth International Congress of Anthropology and Ethnology* 2: 330–40.

———. 1957. "Factionalism at Taos Pueblo, New Mexico." Anthropological Paper No. 56. Washington, D.C.: Smithsonian Institution, Bureau of American Ethnology.

Festinger, Leon. 1957. A theory of cognitive dissonance. Stanford: Stanford Univ. Press.

———. 1964. Conflict, decision, and dissonance. Stanford: Stanford Univ. Press.

Firth, Raymond, "Factions in Indian and overseas societies." *Brit. J. Sociol.* 8: 291–341.

———. 1959. Social change in Tikopia: Restudy of a Polynesian community after a generation. London: Allen & Unwin.

Fortes, Meyer. 1945. The dynamics of a clanship among the Tallensi, being the first part of an analysis of the social structure of a trans-Volta tribe. London: Oxford Univ. Press.

———. 1949. Social structure: Studies presented to A. R. Radcliffe-Brown. Oxford: The Clarendon Press.

———, and E. E. Evans-Pritchard. 1941. African political systems. London: Oxford Univ. Press.

Foster, George M. 1961. "The dyadic contract: A model for the social structure of a Mexican peasant village." *Amer. Anthrop.* 63: 1173–92.

French, David H. 1948. Factionalism in Isleta Pueblo. Monographs of the AES, No. XIV. Seattle: Univ. of Washington Press.

———. 1962. "Ambiguity and irrelevancy in factional conflict," in Intergroup relations and leadership, ed. Muzafer Sherif. New York: Wiley.

Gluckman, Max. 1939. "Analysis of a social situation in modern Zululand." *Bantu Stud.* 14: 147–74.

———. 1941. "The kingdom of the Zulu of South Africa," in African political systems, ed. Meyer Fortes and E. E. Evans-Pritchard. London: Oxford Univ. Press.

———. 1954. Rituals of rebellion in Southeast Africa. Manchester: Manchester Univ. Press.

———. 1955. Custom and conflict in Africa. Glencoe, Ill.: Free Press.

———, ed. 1962. Essays on ritual of social relations, by Daryll Ford and others. Manchester: Manchester Univ. Press.

Goldfrank, Esther S. 1943. "Historic change and social character: A study of the Teton Dakota." *Amer. Anthrop.* 45: 67–83.

Gulliver, P. H. 1961. "Land shortage, social change, and social conflict in East Africa." *J. Conflict Resolution* 5: 16–26.

Hackett, C. W., and C. C. Shelby. 1942. Revolt of the Pueblo Indians of New Mexico and Otermin's attempted reconquest, 1680–82.

176 *Bibliography*

Coronado Historical Series, Vols. VIII and IX. Albuquerque: Univ. of New Mexico Press.

Hammond, G. P. 1926. Don Juan de Onate and the founding of New Mexico. *New Mexico Hist. Rev.*, 1: 42–77 and 2: 156–92.

——, and A. Rey. 1927. The Gallegos relation of the Rodriguez expedition to New Mexico. Publications in History, Vol. IV. Santa Fe: Historical Society of New Mexico.

——, and A. Rey. 1929. Expedition into New Mexico by Antonio de Espejo, 1582–83, as revealed in the journal of Diego Perez de Luzan, a member of the party. Los Angeles: The Quivera Society.

Hodge, F. W., G. P. Hammond, and A. Rey. 1945. Revised memorial of Alonzo de Benavides, 1634. Coronado Historical Series, Vol. IV. Albuquerque: Univ. of New Mexico Press.

Homans, George C. 1950. The human group. New York: Harcourt Brace.

The Inquiry. 1929. Community conflict (preliminary edition). New York: The Inquiry.

Kluckhohn, Clyde. 1953. Personality in nature, society, and culture. 2nd ed. rev. and enlarged by K. and Henry Murray with David M. Schneider. New York: Knopf.

Kopytoff, Igor. 1961. "Extension of conflict as a method of conflict resolution among the Suku of the Congo." *J. Conflict Resolution* 5: 61–69.

Kornhauser, Arthur W., Robert Dubin, and Arthur M. Ross, eds. 1954. Industrial conflict. New York: McGraw-Hill.

Krige, E. Jensen, and J. D. Krige. 1943. The realm of a rain queen. New York: Oxford Univ. Press.

Kuper, Hilda. 1947. An African aristocracy. London: Oxford Univ. Press.

——. 1964. The Swazi, a South African kingdom. New York: Holt, Rinehart, and Winston.

Lasswell, Harold D. 1935. "Faction," in Encyclopedia of the social sciences, ed. Edwin R. A. Seligman. New York: Macmillan.

Leinster, Murray. 1957. Colonial survey. New York: Gnome.

Lessa, William A. 1964. "The social effects of Typhoon Ophelia (1960) on Ulithi." *Micronesia*, Vol. 1, Nos. 1 and 2.

LeVine, Robert A., ed. 1961. "Anthropology and the study of conflict: An introduction." *J. conflict Resolution* 5:3–15.

Lewis, Oscar. 1951. Life in a Mexican village: Tepoztlan restudied. Urbana: Univ. of Illinois Press.

——, with Harvant Singh Dhillon. 1954. Group dynamics in a

North Indian village: A study of factions. New Delhi: Programme Evaluation Organization Planning Commission, Government of India.

———, with Victor Barnouw. 1958. Village life in North India. Urbana: Univ. of Illinois Press.

Linton, Ralph. 1933. The Tanala, a hill tribe of Madagascar. Chicago: Field Museum of Natural History.

———, ed. 1940. Acculturation in seven American Indian tribes. New York: Appleton-Century.

Marriott, McKim. 1960. Caste ranking and community structure in five regions of India and Pakistan. Deccan College Monograph Series, No. 23. Poona: Deccan College Postgraduate and Research Institute.

McFee, Malcolm. 1957. "Factionalism in three southwestern American Indian communities." Unpublished Master's thesis, Stanford Univ.

Mead, George Herbert. 1959. Mind, self, and society. Chicago: Univ. of Chicago Press.

Metzger, Duane. 1960. "Conflict in Chulsanto." *Alpha Kappa Deltan, A Sociological Journal* 30: 35–48.

Mills, Theodore M. 1964. Group transformation: An analysis of a learning group. Englewood Cliffs, N.J.: Prentice-Hall.

Murdock, George Peter. 1949. Social structure. New York: Macmillan.

Murphy, Robert F. 1961. Deviancy and social control I: What makes Biboi run? *Kroeber Anthrop. Soc. Pap.* 24: 55–61.

Nader, L. J., and Duane Metzger. 1963. "Conflict resolution in two Mexican communities." *Amer. Anthrop.* 65: 584–92.

Nehnevajsa, Jiri. 1957. "Some notes on factionalism in the Soviet Union." *Internat. J. Sociometry,* 1: 145–50.

Nicholas, Ralph W. 1963. "Village factions and political parties in rural West Bengal." *J. Commonwealth Political Stud.* 2: 17–32.

North, Robert C. 1962. "International conflict and integration: Problems of research," in Intergroup relations and leadership, ed. Muzafer Sherif. New York: Wiley.

———, Howard E. Koch, Jr., and Dina Zinnes. 1960. "The integrative functions of conflict." *J. Conflict Resolution,* IV, No. 3, 355–84.

Parsons, Elsie C. 1936. Taos Pueblo. Menasha, Wis.: American Anthropologist.

———. 1939. Pueblo Indian religion. Chicago: Univ. of Chicago Press.

Parsons, Talcott, and Edward A. Shils. 1951. Toward a general theory of action. Cambridge: Harvard Univ. Press.

Pelto, Pertti J., and John MacGregor. 1963. "Competition and hostility in little communities." Paper presented at the 62nd annual meeting of the AAA, San Francisco.

Pierson, Donald. 1948. "Cruz das Almas: a Brazilian village." Anthropological Paper No. 12. Washington, D.C.: Smithsonian Institution, Institute of Social Anthropology.

Pitt-Rivers, George Henry Lane-Fox. 1927. The clash of culture and the contact of races. London: George Routledge.

Pocock, David. 1957. "The bases of faction in Gujerat," in "Factions in Indian and overseas societies." *Brit. J. Sociol.* 8: 291–341.

Redfield, Robert, and Alfonso Villa Rojas. 1962 (1st ed. 1934). Chan Kom, a Maya village. Chicago: Univ. of Chicago Press.

Reed, Nelson. 1964. The caste war of Yucatan. Stanford: Stanford Univ. Press.

Sahlins, Marshall D. 1962. Moala culture and nature on a Fijian island. Ann Arbor: Univ. of Michigan Press.

Sapir, Edward. 1924. "Culture, genuine and spurious." *Amer. J. Sociol.* 30: 401–29.

Scholes, F. V. 1930. "The supply service of the New Mexico missions in the seventeenth century." *New Mexico Hist. Rev.* 5: 93–115, 186–98.

———. 1935. "Civil government and society in New Mexico in the seventeenth century." *New Mexico Hist. Rev.* 10: 71–111.

———. 1942. Troublous times in New Mexico, 1659–70. Publications in History, Vol. II. Albuquerque: Historical Society of New Mexico.

Siegel, Bernard J. 1949. "Some observations on the pueblo pattern at Taos." *Amer. Anthrop.* 51: 567.

———. 1961. "Conflict, parochialism, and social differentiation in Portuguese society." *J. Conflict Resolution* 5: 35–42.

Simmel, Georg. 1955. Conflict (tr. Kurt H. Wolff) and The web of group affiliations (tr. Reinhard Bendix). Glencoe, Ill.: Free Press.

Sorokin, Pitirim. 1937–41. Social and cultural dynamics. New York: American Book Co.

Spicer, E. H. 1940. Pascua, a Yaqui village in Arizona. Chicago: Univ. of Chicago Press.

Spoehr, Alexander. 1949. Majuro: A village in the Marshall Islands. (Fieldiana: *Anthropology*, Vol. 39.) Chicago: Natural History Museum.

Srinivas, M. N. 1955. "The social system of a Mysore village," in Village India, Memoir No. 83 of the AAA, McKim Marriott, ed. Chicago: Univ. of Chicago Press.

Tobin, J. E. 1953. "An investigation of the sociopolitical schism on Majuro Atoll." Majuro: Marshall Islands. Mimeo.

Toufic, Touma. 1958. Un village de montagne au Liban (Hadeth el-Jobbé). Le monde d'outre-mer passé et présent. 3d Series Essays. Paris: Ecole Pratique des Hautes Etudes, VIème section.

Turner, Victor W. 1957. Schism and continuity in an African society: A study of Ndembu village life. New York: Humanities Press.

Useem, John. 1949. Report on Palau. Coordinated investigation of Micronesian anthropology, report 21. Office of Naval Research and National Academy of Sciences.

Vanstone, James W. 1962. Point Hope, an Eskimo village in transition. Seattle: Univ. of Washington Press.

Vidich, A. J. 1949. "Political factionalism in Palau." Washington, D.C.: Pacific Science Board and National Research Council. Mimeo.

Wallace, Anthony F. C. 1961. Culture and personality. New York: Random House.

Whitman, William. Ed. Marjorie W. Whitman. 1947. The Pueblo Indians of San Ildefonso, a changing culture. New York: Columbia Univ. Press.

Wilson, Godfrey, and Monica Wilson. 1945. The analysis of social change based on observations in Central Africa. Cambridge: Cambridge Univ. Press.

Winship, G. P. 1896. "The Coronado expedition, 1540–42," in Fourteenth annual report, Bureau of American Ethnology. Washington, D.C.: Smithsonian Institution.

Index